Prince **Harry**

Royal Rule-Breaker

By Elizabeth Krajnik

Portions of this book originally appeared in
Prince Harry by Cherese Cartlidge.

P R E S S

Published in 2020 by
Lucent Press, an Imprint of Greenhaven Publishing, LLC
353 3rd Avenue
Suite 255
New York, NY 10010

Designer: Deanna Paternostro
Editor: Elizabeth Krajnik

Cataloging-in-Publication Data

Names: Krajnik, Elizabeth.
Title: Prince Harry: royal rule-breaker / Elizabeth Krajnik.
Description: New York : Lucent Press, 2020. | Series: People in the news |
Includes index.
Identifiers: ISBN 9781534567672 (pbk.) | ISBN 9781534567047 (library bound) |
ISBN 9781534567689 (ebook)
Subjects: LCSH: Harry, Prince, Duke of Sussex, 1984—Juvenile literature. | Princes-
-Great Britain–Biography–Juvenile literature.
Classification: LCC DA591.A45 K73 2020 | DDC 941.086092 B–dc23

Printed in the United States of America

CPSIA compliance information: Batch #BS19KL: For further information contact Greenhaven Publishing LLC, New York,
New York, at 1-844-317-7404.

Please visit our website, www.greenhavenpublishing.com. For a free color
catalog of all our high-quality books, call toll free 1-844-317-7404 or fax
1-844-317-7405.

Contents

Foreword

We live in a world where the latest news is always available and where it seems we have unlimited access to the lives of the people in the news. Entire television networks are devoted to news about politics, sports, and entertainment. Social media has allowed people to have an unprecedented level of interaction with celebrities. We have more information at our fingertips than ever before. However, how much do we really know about the people we see on television news programs, social media feeds, and magazine covers?

Despite the constant stream of news, the full stories behind the lives of some of the world's most newsworthy men and women are often unknown. Who was Gal Gadot before she became Wonder Woman? What does LeBron James do when he is not playing basketball? What inspires Lin-Manuel Miranda?

This series aims to answer questions like these about some of the biggest names in pop culture, sports, politics, and technology. While the subjects of this series come from all walks of life and areas of expertise, they share a common magnetism that has made them all captivating figures in the public eye. They have shaped the world in some unique way, and—in many cases—they are poised to continue to shape the world for many years to come.

These biographies are not just a collection of basic facts. They tell compelling stories that show how each figure grew to become a powerful public personality. Each book aims to paint a complete, realistic picture of its subject—from the challenges they overcame to the controversies they caused. In doing so, each book reinforces the idea that even the most famous faces on the news are real people who are much more complex than we are often shown in brief video clips or sound bites. Readers are also reminded that there is even more to a person than what they present to the world through social media posts, press releases, and interviews. The whole story of a person's life can only be discovered by digging beneath the surface of their public persona, and that is what this series allows readers to do.

The books in this series are filled with enlightening quotes from speeches and interviews given by the subjects, as well as quotes and anecdotes from those who know their story best: family, friends, coaches, and colleagues. All quotes are noted to provide guidance for further research. Detailed lists of additional resources are also included, as are timelines, indexes, and unique photographs. These text features come together to enhance the reading experience and encourage readers to dive deeper into the stories of these influential men and women.

Fame can be fleeting, but the subjects featured in this series have real staying power. They have fundamentally impacted their respective fields and have achieved great success through hard work and true talent. They are men and women defined by their accomplishments, and they are often seen as role models for the next generation. They have left their mark on the world in a major way, and their stories are meant to inspire readers to leave their mark, too.

Sixth in Line

Prince Harry, Duke of Sussex, is the younger son of Charles, Prince of Wales, and the late Diana, Princess of Wales. He is one of the most famous royals living today. From early on, Harry and his older brother, William, have been in the spotlight. After Clarence House, the official residence of the Prince of Wales and the Duchess of Cornwall, announced Prince Harry's engagement to American actress and divorcée Meghan Markle on November 27, 2017, his life was thrust even further into the spotlight. Prince Harry and Meghan Markle were married on May 19, 2018. More than 50 million people in the United States and Britain alone watched the wedding.

Harry's full name is Henry Charles Albert David. He and the rest of his father's side are members of the House of Windsor. This family name was adopted in 1917 after King George V proclaimed the British royal family's name would be changed. As of early 2019, the Windsor monarch is Queen Elizabeth II, who has been ruling since June 2, 1953. She is married to Prince Philip, Duke of Edinburgh, whose name is Philip Mountbatten and was born Prince Philip of Greece and Denmark. Sometimes Prince Harry uses Mountbatten-Windsor as his last name if one is required. However, while serving in the British army he was known as Captain Harry Wales. He has used Wales as his surname in the

Prince Harry served in the British army for 10 years. He rose to the rank of captain and completed two tours of duty in Afghanistan.

past because it is the area over which his father is prince.

As of early 2019, Prince Harry is sixth in the line of succession to the throne. Previously, he was only third in line after

William and Charles. However, since the birth of William's children—Prince George, Princess Charlotte, and Prince Louis—Prince Harry has been bumped down in the line. This means he is also sixth in line as Supreme Governor of the Church of England.

Following Tradition

For centuries, monarchies have used the "heir and a spare" system to ensure power would stay in their families. Power was usually passed on from male to male, and therefore, each ruling family needed to have two sons: one to rule and another to take his place if he died. This system remains today, but with the advent of modern medicine, the likelihood of the eldest child dying is much less. By having an heir and a spare, Prince Charles and Princess Diana were following tradition to ensure the survival and continuation of the House of Windsor.

Prince Harry was born on September 15, 1984, and the world quickly began referring to the princes William and Harry as "the heir and the spare." Prince Charles is the heir apparent. This means that, as the eldest son of a reigning monarch, he is first in line to the throne and his place as future king cannot be usurped by the birth of another male heir. William is second in the line of succession to the throne, and it is his duty to take over as king after his father. As Charles's eldest son, William's place as future king also cannot be usurped, which makes him an heir apparent as well. Harry is the heir presumptive, which means that his place in the line of succession to the throne can change. Before Prince William and Kate Middleton had their children, Harry was third in the line of succession to the throne. With the birth of each child, Harry has been bumped down in the line.

Prince Harry shared the experience of being a second son with his uncle: Prince Andrew, Duke of York. Andrew was second in line to the throne after Charles until he was 22 years old, when Prince William was born. Andrew then became third in line, and, after Harry's birth, fourth. As of 2019, Prince Andrew is seventh in the line of succession to the throne.

While many stated that Harry's royal purpose when he was a child was to take William's place as king if something happened, today, his royal purpose is much different. In order for Harry to become the next king of England, something would have to happen to Prince Charles, Prince William, and all of William's children.

William's Shadow

Growing up, Prince William often cast a shadow over Prince Harry. Although being a member of the royal family means being thrust into the spotlight, Harry often felt that what he did did not matter as much as what William did. Why should what he do matter? William was going to be the one who would become

It is an unspoken rule that royals are not allowed to show public displays of affection. Prince Harry, however, has challenged this rule from very early on. Prince Harry and his then girlfriend Chelsy Davy are pictured here kissing at the ICC Cricket World Cup 2007 Super Eight match between England and Australia on April 8, 2007.

king one day. As a teen and young adult, Harry was sometimes the subject of sensational tabloid headlines for engaging in wild behavior. He got caught naked in Las Vegas, Nevada; drank champagne out of a prosthetic leg; tried to fight paparazzi outside a nightclub; kissed his girlfriends in public; and stayed up until the early hours of the morning and jumped off a balcony on the day of Prince William's wedding. Because Harry does not have the same heavy responsibilities as William, there has been more room for him to get away with reckless and wild behavior than there has been for William. Harry has more freedom to behave the way he wants because, as Harry explained, "William's got—well, we've both got our lives set out, but I think he's got his life *really* set out."[1]

Like the rest of the British royal family, Prince Harry is recognized throughout the world, wherever he goes, and has been all his life. In fact, it is rare that he can just blend in when he is in public. He is constantly followed and photographed, even when he is trying to relax. Speaking of his past actions, Prince Harry has said, "Yes, I'm not normal. As much as I'd like to be normal, I'm not normal . . . Unfortunately William and I can't be normal."[2] Normalcy, unfortunately, is not a possibility for the royal family when every aspect of their lives comes under the scrutiny of the general public.

Even though Harry has gotten into trouble in the past, he has since matured and grown into a man who has the respect of his people. Despite his royal status, he is modest. He has said, "I am who I am, though I believe I'm no one special."[3] Today, Prince Harry remains something of a maverick, insisting on doing things his own way.

Chapter One

The Early Years

Growing up as young royals was not easy for William and Harry. However, Prince Charles and Princess Diana did all they could to give their sons some semblance of a normal childhood. Like normal children, William and Harry attended school and had other experiences many children have. However, they also went on official royal visits from a young age. Both of the boys formed close relationships with their parents. However, their parents' divorce and Princess Diana's death had a lasting impact on them.

A Second Son Is Born

His Royal Highness Prince Henry Charles Albert David of Wales was born at 4:20 p.m. on September 15, 1984, at St. Mary's Hospital, Paddington, in central London. His father, Prince Charles, was in the delivery room when Harry arrived that afternoon. Newborn Harry had light blue eyes and a little bit of reddish hair. Immediately after Harry's birth, Charles called his mother, the queen of England, to tell her the news. Then, he drove back to Kensington Palace to tell William about his new baby brother.

News outlets throughout the world announced Harry's birth. The Prince and Princess of Wales had now produced the heir and the spare, thereby ensuring the continuation of the House of Windsor. To celebrate the birth of the "spare heir," numerous commemorative souvenirs were issued, including china mugs, thimbles, china dolls, tea towels, and postcards. Well-wishers sent presents for Harry and his parents, including flowers, balloons, telegrams, and toys. Many celebrities also sent gifts. Singer Barry Manilow sent a miniature antique baby grand piano, while pop star Michael Jackson sent a stuffed monkey toy and a card.

As a baby, Prince Harry had a more demure nature. According to Prince Charles, baby Harry was easy to take care of—every parent's dream baby. He said Harry was "extraordinarily good, sleeps marvelously and eats well." He added that Harry was "the

Princess Diana is shown here on the steps of St. Mary's Hospital with Prince Harry in her arms and Prince Charles by her side the day after Harry was born.

one with the gentle nature,"[4] whereas William was the boisterous one. Indeed, Harry was a quiet baby. Prince Harry was christened by the Archbishop of Canterbury, Robert Runcie, at St. George's Chapel in Windsor on December 21, 1984. One of the choirboys recalled that Harry cried for only about two or three minutes and "was as quiet as a mouse throughout the rest."[5]

The Bonds of Brotherhood

Being William's younger brother often meant that Harry was overlooked. As a child, Harry sometimes felt like he was invisible or did not matter because people would make a fuss over his brother and ignore him. However, Prince Charles and Princess Diana did their best to make sure he never felt like he came second to William in their eyes. While pregnant with Harry, for example, Princess Diana went shopping for new baby clothes and toys even though Charles suggested they just use William's hand-me-downs.

One of the ways Diana tried to make Harry feel important was by involving him in William's life—and William in his. While she was pregnant, Princess Diana encouraged William to bond with the new baby by touching her stomach. When William, who was just two years old, first met Harry on the morning after he was born, he kissed Harry's forehead and described his new brother as "the most beautiful thing I have ever seen."[6] William's affection for his baby brother continued after Harry was brought home from the hospital. "Harry was his favorite toy,"[7] Diana confessed. She recalled family time when Harry was an infant: "William spends the entire time pouring an endless supply of hugs and kisses on Harry and we are hardly allowed near."[8] As they got older, Diana always made sure Harry was included in William's activities and was in the picture whenever his brother was photographed.

Partly as a result of their mother's efforts to involve them in each other's lives, Harry and William became extremely close. They were—and still are—each other's best friend and share a very strong bond. William was very protective of his little brother, and Harry, in turn, worshipped his big brother and tried to emulate him. This was sometimes very cute, but other times,

Prince Harry (left) and Prince William (right) often had their photos taken while on vacation.

it could be difficult for Prince Charles and Princess Diana to cope with.

As a young child, Harry would often climb into bed with William during the night. He could not bear to be apart from his brother, and Harry struggled when William went off to nursery school. Eventually, Diana let Harry come along when she accompanied William to school so he could spend a few extra minutes with his big brother.

Harry and William have loved all kinds of physical activities—including swimming, skiing, tennis, polo, and rugby—since they were young. At an early age, it became obvious that, even though William was very athletic, Harry was better at sports. "The sporting star of the family is definitely Harry, and it always has been," said journalist Ingrid Seward. "And that used to really irritate William, because he would see his younger brother better on the skis than he was. And Harry was fearless."[9]

Growing Up "Normal"

Despite having extensive royal duties, Prince Charles and Princess Diana were devoted to spending as much time as possible with their children. They wanted to give William and Harry a "normal" childhood, and Diana in particular took special care to make this happen. She made sure they had plenty of chances to play with ordinary kids in a normal social setting. She also dressed them in regular, everyday clothes such as jeans, sweatshirts, and baseball caps, rather than the matching suits or traditional sailor outfits worn by the children of many royals.

Most of all, Diana wanted Harry and William to have fun and enjoy their childhood before they became adults and took on the heavy responsibilities that come with their royal positions. She made sure they got to enjoy fast-food hamburgers at restaurants like McDonald's and Burger King. She never asked for or accepted any special treatment when she took the boys there, and she insisted they wait in line like everybody else.

In an effort to raise the boys normally, Diana taught them not to take advantage of people because they were royal. However, it is impossible to disregard the fact that the royal family is very wealthy. Highgrove House, Charles and Diana's country home, boasted nine main bedrooms, four reception rooms, a nursery wing, and staff quarters. Servants included butlers, a housekeeper, a chef, a nanny, and several personal attendants. Because she could afford to buy her sons whatever they wanted, Diana showered them with gifts. Harry and William grew up with all the latest technology, and, like most kids their age, they loved playing computer games and had a large collection of all the latest games. The boys also had their own Shetland ponies, as well as a scaled-down replica of a Jaguar automobile.

Prince Harry's and Prince William's ponies' names were Smokey and Trigger. They sometimes brought the ponies with them to the royal family's many residences.

Royal Residences

When Harry was growing up, the royal family had two main residences they split their time between. Their London home was Kensington Palace, which was built in the early 17th century. The family's apartment at Kensington had a rooftop garden, which the family often used for barbeques. The boys shared an attic room that was converted into a nursery, which featured furniture with hand-painted animals and cartoon characters. The big room had yellow walls filled with bookcases and toy cabinets. It also had a wooden rocking horse that was a gift from Nancy Reagan, wife of then U.S. president Ronald Reagan. The boys ate their meals in the nursery, and Diana often joined them. She and Charles would also attend tea parties in the nursery that William put on, while Harry would run around.

Harry felt happiest at Highgrove House. It was built in 1796 and is located on 348 wooded acres (141 ha) about two hours' drive west of London. Some of Harry's earliest memories are of playing in Highgrove House's walled garden. Like the rest of his immediate family, young Harry had a great love of the outdoors and of animals. The family went to Highgrove as often as possible. Charles wanted to pass on his love of traditional country activities, such as hunting and shooting, to the boys.

Coming Second

Prince Charles and Princess Diana did their best to combat Harry's feelings of inadequacy to William. Even though he was the spare, they never wanted him to feel like he was in second place. To make Harry feel equal, they made sure he and William had the same opportunities. Richard Kay, a British journalist and close friend of Diana's, explained,

She worried, because he was the number two, that he would be the one who would be overlooked. Everyone would come to William; William was the one they were grooming for the future. And it was one of the reasons why Diana used to say ... that she wanted to involve Harry in William's life. And it carries on to this day. William rarely does photo calls on his own. Harry is always drawn into those, because she didn't want him to be constantly overlooked—"Oh, he's the spare, he doesn't count." She wanted him to count.[1]

1. *Harry: The Mysterious Prince.* DVD. Directed by Alan Scales. London, UK: BBC. Worldwide/ Infinity, 2005.

Highgrove is where William and Harry learned to ride horses. As the older of the two, William learned before Harry. When they were younger, the boys rode the Shetland ponies gifted to them—Smokey and Trigger. When William was about three or four years old, someone would lead him around on his pony and Harry would watch from the sidelines. When he was too small to ride on his own, Harry would sometimes get to sit in the saddle with William while the pony stood still. However, Harry would cry when he was taken off the pony to let William ride on his own.

The royal family spent a great deal of time at Highgrove House before the boys began their schooling. There they were able to play like normal children.

Harry and William loved exploring the grounds at Highgrove. The estate features Duchy Home Farm, which is an organic working farm on the property set up by Prince Charles in 1985. Today, Home Farm has British breeds of pigs, cattle, and sheep. When they were little, the boys helped care for the rabbits and guinea pigs that also lived there and got to watch lambs being sheared. A favorite game was to run into a farm field shouting at the top of their lungs and make all the cows and sheep run away. The weekends spent at Highgrove were happy, carefree times for the young family.

Unconventional Royal Parenting

Traditionally, royal parenting has consisted of nannies taking much of the weight off the parents' shoulders. Unlike many other royals before her, including Queen Elizabeth II, Diana was a very hands-on mother who insisted on doing things like driving the boys to school herself. Ken Wharfe, a police bodyguard who protected Diana and her two sons for seven years, recalled that Diana never missed a single day unless it was absolutely unavoidable. "The opportunity to talk through their school day with 'Mummy' on the short car journey from Kensington Palace to both kindergarten at Jane Mynors's and pre-prep [pre-preparatory school] at the Wetherby School was an invaluable time for the boys," he said. "Both William and Harry loved this aspect of their mother's involvement."[10]

Diana encouraged the boys' interests and often joined them in playing games and honing their athleticism. For example, she would be goalkeeper for their soccer matches on the lawn at Kensington Palace. In 1993, Diana took William and Harry to Walt Disney World in Florida, which was one of their favorite vacations. "When the boys were very young," Diana said, "I just remember life being one long laugh whenever they were there."[11] Both boys adored their mother and loved spending hours watching TV and having somewhat unfair tickle fights, which the boys almost always won.

As a young boy, Harry was quite attached to Princess Diana, constantly seeking her out for affection and attention. Writer

Judy Wade described him as "a terribly affectionate little boy, always wrapped around his mother, sneaking into her bed early in the morning for a cuddle."[12] Harry was also somewhat jealous of William and would often retaliate if he saw William getting preferential treatment. Ingrid Seward recounted, "When Harry was younger, he was jealous of William because he wanted his mother all to himself. If they were in a room together, Harry would sit almost on top of Diana in his anxiety to be close to her."[13]

Father-Son Relationship

Even though Harry was very close with Princess Diana, he also had a good relationship with Prince Charles. Time spent at Highgrove provided opportunities for Charles and Harry to form their father-son relationship. "Harry loves animals and plants," Charles once said. "I tell him all about them and say they have feelings, too, and mustn't be hurt."[14] Harry had his own set of garden tools, which he used to help his father. Just like his father, he would talk to plants—and sometimes to himself. Harry cherished these summer afternoons spent with Charles. In the evenings after hours of digging, Charles and Harry would sit on a garden bench with glasses of juice and talk as the sun set, staying on the bench until it got too dark to see.

When the boys were young, Charles was a hands-on parent. He loved to spend time with the boys, playing games, horseback riding, and hunting. Charles also read to both boys when they were young. A favorite book was C.S. Lewis's *The Lion, the Witch, and the Wardrobe*. When Harry began reading, Charles listened patiently as his son sounded out the words. Harry inherited his father's love of reading. Harry would look around for a new book to borrow from Charles's personal library at Highgrove House. One of Harry's favorite authors while he was growing up was Stephen King, an American horror novelist.

At Balmoral Castle in Scotland, Harry and his father would take long walks in the mornings across the estate's misty fields. They would discuss their plans for the day: shooting or hunting. Harry started going grouse hunting with his dad at age nine and soon became a good shot.

Money Matters

British money is similar to American money in that it features the face of a prominent national figure—Queen Elizabeth II. However, because the queen is the princes' grandmother, that adds a level of familiarity no other British people possess. When Harry and William were young children, Diana taught the boys to call money a "granny." Because different denominations of the British pound (£) are different colors, £5 notes were "blue grannies," £10 notes were "brown grannies," and £50 notes were "pink grannies." Being given spending money is a common part of life for many nonroyal children, and the boys enjoyed having a unique way of referring to such a mundane part of British life. When Diana asked them how much spending money they needed, William would always ask for a pink granny. The princes continued referring to pound notes this way well into adulthood.

A Royal Schoolboy

In September 1987, Harry set out for his first day of school at Mrs. Mynors' Nursery School in west London—the same nursery school Prince William had attended. At that point, William had already begun his education at the Wetherby School. The three-year-old was not very happy about going to school. On his first day, Harry cried and clung to Diana the entire 10-minute ride from Kensington Palace to the school. Once inside, he became very quiet and reserved and cried when his parents left. "I had a lump in my throat when we left Harry,"[15] Charles recalled. When Harry first started school, he was shy and kept to himself. However, after a few weeks, Harry adjusted and came out of his shell.

At school, Harry showed some natural leadership abilities, often taking charge in a game of follow the leader. One of his favorite activities at the school was painting. He loved expressing himself freely with paint and crayons, and he frequently got paint splattered all over his clothes.

When Harry was five years old, he began attending the same school as William. In September 1989, he joined his brother at Wetherby School, a pre-preparatory school for boys two and a half to eight years old. Harry was a bright student. One member of Prince Charles's staff described young Harry as "a walking encyclopedia—he positively loved learning new things, any scrap of information interested him as long as it was something new."[16]

At Wetherby, some of Harry's favorite classes were art and English. He enjoyed painting and model making, and he loved to write stories. Harry's teachers considered him to be a gifted writer. However, Harry's favorite thing at Wetherby was performing. He had acting roles in plays and sang in the choir. At just six years old, he was good at memorizing lines and often earned the lead role in school plays, including *The Lion, the Witch, and the Wardrobe*.

Growing to Love the Military

As it often happens, young children outgrow their stuffed animals and pursue new interests. By the time Harry was five years old, he began showing an interest in everything military related. He loved playing with his toy soldiers and tank. He also had a specially made replica uniform from the Parachute Regiment, which he loved wearing when he played soldier.

The 1964 film *Zulu* greatly impacted Harry's life. It depicts the real-life Battle of Rorke's Drift in South Africa in 1879, a 10-hour battle during which about 100 British soldiers held off attacks from about 4,000 Zulu warriors. Harry was fascinated by the movie and asked his father question after question about the battle. When Prince Charles promised to take him one day to visit the home base of the South Wales Borderers—the regiment involved in the Battle at Rorke's Drift—Harry was thrilled.

A number of Harry's family members have been in the military. When he was younger, Harry liked to ask them questions about their military experiences. Charles is colonel-in-chief of 14 regiments, and his various dress uniforms fascinated Harry. Ken Wharfe recalled that Harry seemed obsessed with soldiers and the army. According to Wharfe, "Every birthday or Christmas, whenever Harry was asked what he wanted for his main present, his response was always the same: 'An army uniform—I really need a camouflage jacket.'"[17]

Harry spent a great deal of time on trips with Diana. In 1993, Princess Diana took Prince Harry to visit the barracks of the Light Dragoons, a light cavalry regiment in the Adaptive Force of the

On July 12, 1993, racing legend Jackie Stewart (second from left) led Prince Harry (center) around the track at the British Grand Prix at Silverstone in London, England. For a brief time, Harry wanted to be a Formula One driver.

British army, in Hanover, Germany. During their visit, Harry got to wear a replica uniform and ride in a tank. Even though Diana took Harry on other trips that played into his other interests, such as Formula One racing, the military remained Harry's passion. His love for the military from a young age influenced his future in a number of ways.

Chapter Two

Growing Up Fast

Prince Harry gradually became much more outgoing. His bold and fun-loving personality had the chance to shine. Harry's behavior was occasionally reckless, dangerous, and reflected poorly on his family. However, Harry tried to be a good person and to stay strong during many hard times in his life. Despite his behavior getting him in trouble from time to time, as Prince Harry grew up, he remained a sensitive, perceptive, and pleasant young man. The trials in Harry's personal life took a great toll on him and William. The royal family was thrust even further into the media spotlight in these years, and Harry had to work hard to protect his family's image.

The Fearless Prince

As a young boy, Harry enjoyed pushing his boundaries. His fearlessness sometimes got him in trouble, and on occasion, what began as innocent fun became reckless endangerment. One of Harry's favorite games was to chase cows in the fields at Highgrove House. On one occasion, Harry was chasing a cow, and it headed straight for Princess Diana. To avoid getting trampled, Diana jumped over a fence, which was amusing to Harry. Another one of Harry and William's favorite activities was setting up a roadblock

In important situations, Harry had a tendency to act out for the cameras. Here, he is shown sticking his tongue out while on the balcony of Buckingham Palace on June 11, 1988.

on the Highgrove estate and requiring staff and police guards to pay a toll to pass. When Harry would take the game too far and throw stones at people who could not pay the toll, William would step in and stop him from misbehaving. His behavior prompted Diana's brother, Earl Spencer, to refer to Harry as a "mischievous imp."[18]

Harry's behavior sometimes embarrassed his family. Even though his behavior may have been cute when he was younger, Harry's parents were concerned a tabloid would catch their son—who was often in the spotlight—doing something inappropriate in public. As a royal, Harry's behavior had to be of a higher caliber than that of nonroyal children. Because Harry was a royal, his wild behavior had the potential to embarrass the monarchy.

Other times, Harry got injured as a result of his fearlessness. Just before his second birthday, Harry leapt off the kitchen table. He hit his head and needed stitches, which left a scar. This disregard for danger did not lessen as Harry got older. In fact, Harry only became more fearless as time went by. For example, he and William had go-karts they loved to ride around the grounds at

A Mischievous Young Royal

Harry's obsession with the military got him in trouble, too. It was not uncommon for him to beg the royal bodyguards to show him their guns and let him use their radios. One day, Ken Wharfe finally gave in and allowed Prince Harry, who was just seven years old, to take the radio to several points within the Kensington Palace compound.

Kensington Palace was guarded 24 hours a day, and Harry had promised to check in with Wharfe via the radio. Wharfe did not think there was any harm in letting Harry have some fun. All went well at first, but when it was time for Harry to radio in from one of the checkpoints Wharfe had set up, a police barrier, Harry did not radio. The officer at the barrier told Wharfe that Harry had not been seen.

Wharfe was unable to contact Prince Harry and became panicked. However, Harry finally radioed him to let him know he was all right. Harry had snuck off the Kensington Palace grounds and went to Tower Records on Kensington's High Street. Wharfe ran to get him and bring him back to the palace.

Highgrove, sometimes going as fast as 30 miles (48 km) per hour. After watching nine-year-old Harry try to take a corner at that speed and nearly wipe out, Charles put an end to go-karting in the countryside.

On more than one occasion, Harry's interest in shooting put the lives of other people in danger. When Harry was 11 years old on a shoot on the queen's estate at Sandringham, he fired at a low-flying bird. The bullet whizzed past a helper's head, missing him by inches. Another time, when Harry was 12 years old, he was photographed firing a shotgun out of the sunroof of a moving car while standing in the passenger seat at Windsor Castle.

Each year on December 26, the royal family holds a shoot on the Sandringham estate in Norfolk.

The tabloids got a hold of those photographs and printed them the next day.

Harry was a stubborn young man, and his stubbornness coupled with his fearlessness often got him into trouble. Another occasion almost ended in utter ruin. When Prince Charles was teaching a young Harry how to drive in his Range Rover at Highgrove House, in opposition to the car being put away, Harry reached his foot over and stomped down on the accelerator, causing the car to collide head first with a stone wall. Luckily, no one was hurt, and the car was undamaged. Incidents such as this caused Harry's bodyguards to keep an especially close eye on him. "There was no safe distance with Harry," one of his bodyguards commented. "The combined armies of NATO [the North Atlantic Treaty Organization—an international military force] don't have the destructive force of Harry on a mission to cause mischief."[19]

Charles and Diana

No matter how perfect the royal family's life seemed from the outside, they had their own struggles, like all families. Many people's opinions of Diana put her up on a pedestal. Charles also seemed to be a hands-on father who valued hard work. However, in reality, tensions in their marriage had been building for a long time and inevitably spilled over to affect the boys. In December 1986, unbeknownst to the young princes, Prince Charles had rekindled his relationship with his former girlfriend Camilla Parker Bowles. Charles and Camilla had met through mutual friends at a polo match in 1970. They broke up after Charles joined the Royal Navy, and he eventually began dating and married Diana.

Although Charles and Diana did their best not to fight in front of Harry and William, by early childhood, both boys had picked up on the fact that their parents did not always get along. As time went on, Charles and Diana's constant bickering and fighting was impossible to conceal from the children. The strain on their relationship greatly affected the boys, who turned to each other for comfort during these difficult times. The staff at Highgrove often found the two young boys huddled together on the stairs

A Scandalous Affair

In 1986, Princess Diana began an affair with Captain James Hewitt. In a television interview in 1995, Diana confessed to having an affair with Hewitt until 1991. Immediately, there was a rumor that Harry, who bears a slight resemblance to the redhaired Hewitt, was actually Hewitt's son. Although Diana, Hewitt, and several of Diana's supporters—including Diana's bodyguard, Ken Wharfe—denied that Hewitt was Harry's father owing to the fact that the couple did not even meet until Harry was two years old, the rumor lived on.

Of all the rumors sparked by Diana and Hewitt's affair, Harry was deeply troubled by this rumor more than any other. "Harry has had to live with these stories that he is James Hewitt's son, which he most certainly is not," said British author Judy Wade. "He just happens to have red hair, just like all his cousins on the Spencer side of the family. So, poor Harry is a tormented young man."[1] Over the years, the rumor has resurfaced. As a teen, Harry volunteered to take a DNA test and put an end to the rumors once and for all. However, the queen would not permit it; to allow a paternity test would be to admit that members of the royal family believed there was a possibility Harry may not be a Windsor. In a television interview in 2017, Hewitt suggested that the reason the rumor continues to resurface is because scandal drives tabloid sales.

1. *Harry: The Mysterious Prince*. DVD. Directed by Alan Scales. London, UK: BBC. Worldwide/Infinity, 2005.

with their hands over their ears whenever Charles and Diana were in a heated argument.

When Harry was eight years old, he joined William at Ludgrove School, a boarding school for boys in the countryside near London. Although Harry was glad to be nearer to his brother, the two of them slept in separate dormitories, since they were different ages. At Ludgrove, Harry and William were able to lead somewhat normal lives. They woke up at 7:15 each morning and washed up in a bathroom they shared with the other boys on their floor. After breakfast, Harry went to his classes. In the afternoons, he swam or went to soccer practice. From 6:00 to 8:00 every evening, all the boys were allowed to watch a few educational shows on TV.

Any sense of normalcy the boys had at school soon came to a screeching halt, however. In December 1992, just a few months after Harry started at Ludgrove, Diana arranged to meet with the boys in private. She delivered the heartbreaking news that she and Charles had agreed to formally separate. Upon hearing the news, William broke down in tears, but Harry responded by becoming very quiet, as was typical of him during times of extreme stress.

The news that Charles and Diana's fairy-tale marriage was coming to an end made headlines around the world. Rumors and nasty stories about their bitter separation and divorce were repeated in tabloids and on TV, including speculation that both had affairs. Media coverage only intensified when Charles admitted publicly that he had engaged in a long-term relationship with Camilla Parker Bowles during his marriage. Diana, too, admitted she had carried on a five-year affair with British army captain James Hewitt during her marriage. It seemed the media could not get enough of the salacious details of the failed royal marriage, and there was constant coverage of Harry's parents.

A life without today's forms of social media was not enough to protect the princes from hearing and seeing the rumors being spread about their parents. Teachers and staff at Ludgrove were told not to have their TVs on around students and not to leave newspapers lying about. Despite these efforts, Harry and

William found out what was being said about their parents. William used to sneak into his bodyguard's room and turn on the TV or read the magazines and newspapers there. "I get this sick feeling in my stomach," William said, "every time I see my mother's picture or my father's picture in the newspapers. I know they're going to say something just terrible."[20] William did his best to prevent Harry from seeing the nasty rumors swirling in the media, but even he could not stop Harry from hearing the stories of their parents' problems repeated by the other students.

Harry's performance at Ludgrove underwent a drastic change after his parents' separation. When he first started at Ludgrove, Harry was a hardworking pupil who earned good grades. By the time Harry was 10 years old, he was having trouble concentrating in class. He lost interest in his studies, and his grades began to slip. He often got caught up in what the tabloids were saying about his parents, most of which was completely untrue. This period was very confusing for Harry, who was too young to truly understand what was going on. One teacher at Ludgrove recalled, "Harry just became more and more quiet."[21]

Even though both parents tried to distract the boys from the emotional turmoil surrounding their separation, Harry and William still felt the weight of the situation. The Christmas he was nine, the strain really started to get to him. He and William spent the holiday with their father at Sandringham, and Harry missed his mother profoundly. Two days after Christmas, he went for a long, solitary walk around the estate; a worker who saw him reported that the young prince was "crying his eyes out."[22] No trip or special excursion would be enough to make the princes forget what was really going on—at least not for long. Charles and Diana finalized their divorce in August 1996. Diana received $22.5 million and about $600,000 a year, as well as permission to continue living in her apartment at Kensington Palace. She was stripped of the title "Her Royal Highness" but retained the title "Princess of Wales" and relinquished any future claim to the British throne.

Queen Elizabeth II ordered Prince Charles to divorce Princess Diana rather than continue being married but separated.

The Worst Day of Harry's Life

While vacationing at Balmoral Castle with Prince Charles, Harry's and William's lives changed forever. The princes had not seen their mother for a month and were expecting her to fly home from France on September 1, 1997. Harry, who was two weeks shy of his 13th birthday, missed Diana terribly and could not wait to see her. However, shortly after 7:00 a.m., Harry was woken and given the worst news of his life. On her way home from dinner with her boyfriend Dodi Fayed, Diana's driver, Henri Paul, crashed their car into a part of a tunnel shortly after midnight while attempting to outrun the paparazzi. Paul and Fayed were killed instantly, and Diana and her bodyguard were taken to the hospital. On August 31, 1997, Diana died from the injuries she sustained in the crash. It was later revealed that the driver was intoxicated. Harry was in complete disbelief that his mother had died.

The royal family's first public appearance after Diana's death was when they went to church that Sunday. Diana was not mentioned at that service by request of the royal family. The queen went to great lengths to protect her grandsons from any further heartache. At one point during the church service, Harry leaned over and asked Prince Charles, "Are you sure Mummy is dead?"[23] Going out in public was the last thing Harry wanted to do after his mother died, but he had to put on a brave face as a royal. On September 5, the royal family returned to London for Diana's funeral. Charles took William and Harry to Kensington Palace to look at all the tributes left for their mother.

On September 6, 1997, despite having been stripped of her royal title, Princess Diana was given a royal funeral. As Diana's casket made its way from Kensington Palace to Westminster Abbey,

The decision to have Prince William and Prince Harry walk in Diana's funeral procession was made at the last minute. Prince William was opposed to walking but did it anyway as part of his royal duties.

the immense crowd let out cries of gratitude and wails of sorrow. On top of Diana's casket was an arrangement of white roses and a hand-written card that simply said "Mummy." Harry, William, and Prince Charles came out of their home and were joined by Prince Philip and Princess Diana's brother to walk behind Diana's casket in the funeral procession from St. James's Palace to Westminster Abbey. One of the 1.5 million mourners who lined the 2-mile (3.2 km) route recalled, "As the boys appeared, everybody who was near them averted their eyes. If you had thought about Diana's sons for six days, to look at them now was impossible. People stared at the road, waiting for the coffin to pass."[24] Prince Harry and Prince William kept their composure during what Princess Diana's brother, Charles, Earl Spencer referred to as "a tunnel of grief" and "the most harrowing experience of my life."[25] During all of Diana's funeral proceedings, Harry was determined not to cry in public.

Close Relationships Grow Closer

After his mother's death, Harry's personality changed from being extroverted and easygoing to introverted, and he grew to hate being in the public eye. Harry and William's nanny, a young woman named Tiggy Legge-Bourke, played an important part in calming, comforting, and supporting the young princes in the wake of their mother's tragic deagth. More than anything else, though, it was Harry's close relationship with his father and brother that helped him cope with the loss of his mother.

Prince Charles did his absolute best to help the boys through their grief, despite grieving himself. Harry has expressed amazement that his father was able to be strong in the face of such deep sorrow. In an effort to distract Harry from his sadness, Charles took him on a trip to Africa just two months after Diana's death. Harry enjoyed the time alone with his dad, as well as the change of pace from school. Charles also frequently took both boys skiing, which appealed to Harry's athletic, daredevil nature.

Harry and William's relationship grew even closer. After Diana's death, William became even more protective of Harry. William, who was just 15 years old and mature beyond his years,

William (left), Prince Charles (center), and Harry (right) went on vacation to British Columbia, Canada, in 1998.

worried about how Harry was coping with the loss of their mother, especially when the two returned to school mere days after Diana's funeral. Harry was still at Ludgrove while William had started at Eton College. William called Harry every few days to check up on him.

Harry and William were each other's solid foundations after

Headstrong Harry

Harry and William continue to have a close relationship. Growing up, William's behavior had a profound effect on Harry's. However, William and Harry have distinct personalities, perspectives, and decision-making processes. As future king, William must always consider all viewpoints when making a decision. However, as the "spare" heir, Harry has not had to feel the pressure of being king and therefore has a very different way of thinking. A member of Prince Charles's staff recalled,

> *If [Harry] wants to do something he just goes straight ahead and does it without giving any consideration to the consequences. That's not to say he is a bad boy, he's not. Harry is one of the nicest people you could ever meet, there is nothing he wouldn't do for anyone. Harry's only problem is that he doesn't always think things out. If Harry wants to make a goal for football he'll knock two bits of wood in the ground as posts. ... The fact that the wood has just been pilfered from a royal bench doesn't really faze him.*[1]

1. Quoted in Mark Saunders, *Prince Harry: The Biography*. London, UK: John Blake, 2002, p. 83.

Diana's death, just as they had been during the dissolution of their parents' tormented marriage. "I am unbelievably proud of the two of them," Charles said. "They are really quite remarkable. I think they have handled a very difficult time with enormous courage and the gravest possible dignity."[26] As Harry has explained, he and William are fortunate because "we've got each other to talk to," and that fact is what has seen them through painful times. "We are both very grateful that, you know, each of us were there as a shoulder to cry on if we needed to,"[27] Harry said.

Joining William at Eton College

On September 3, 1998, Harry joined William at Eton College. There, Harry excelled at sports and became a top military cadet. Although Harry struggled somewhat academically, he enjoyed his art classes and participated in the school's drama department. While at Eton, Harry seemed to be a fairly normal young man. His room was decked out with posters, sports equipment, and even a picture of Princess Diana.

However, Harry sometimes engaged in underage drinking at Eton, something to which his bodyguards turned a blind eye. Always within 100 feet (30 m) of the boys, even at school, the bodyguards were under orders not to stop the boys from experiencing a normal adolescence. William was able to keep his antics private and avoid media scrutiny, but Harry was not so fortunate.

In the summer of 2001, when Harry was only sixteen years old, the paparazzi got photos of him drinking in a nightclub in Spain, and pictures of a drunk-looking Harry were published in the British tabloid *News of the World*. Other stories of Harry's indiscretions broke in the tabloids and prompted Prince Charles to address his son's behavior.

Controversy seemed to follow the young prince even after he graduated from Eton in 2003 and began his gap year—a year (or, in Harry's case, two years) taken off after completing school to travel and work abroad before entering the workforce, a university, or the military. In the fall of 2004, a former Eton art teacher claimed that Harry had cheated on his A-level art exam. A-level exams are similar to college entrance exams and are also used for admission to military academies—and Harry desperately wanted a career in the army. The teacher claimed that she had done much of the work for Harry on his art exam, an allegation that made headlines but was never proved. He received a B in his art A-level. After finishing at Eton, Harry began preparing to apply to the Royal Military Academy Sandhurst.

Harry has said that he did not enjoy his years at Eton. However, his time there undoubtedly shaped who he is today.

Harry's Temper

Harry continued to attract attention from the media for his unrestrained behavior. His actions not only affected his reputation as a royal but also as a potential military cadet. In October 2004, as Harry was leaving a London nightclub, a scuffle broke out between him and the paparazzi. The next day, a photo of Harry taking a swing at a photographer was on the front page of a London tabloid, the *Evening Standard*.

It was not the first time Harry had lost his temper in public. On more than one occasion, reporters and paparazzi caught Harry displaying his anger and swearing on the polo field at the Beaufort Polo Club. "He's got the ... Spencer fiery temper," said journalist Richard Kay. "He's on a short fuse, most of the time. And if he's provoked by the sight of photographers or the paparazzi hanging around, he can fly off the handle."[28] Harry's behavior and lack of self-control caused the media and the public to question whether Harry was a lost cause.

One of the most controversial incidents in Prince Harry's early adult life was when a photograph was taken of Harry wearing Nazi insignia at a private costume party in January 2005. Just as with the incident with the photographer outside the nightclub the previous fall, a photograph of Harry in the uniform appeared on the front page of a tabloid the following day, along with the blazing headline "Harry the Nazi."

The reaction was one of widespread shock and horror. Many people thought he should be kept from attending Sandhurst the following year. However, the academy treated Harry as they would any other cadet and permitted him entry. Harry was publicly condemned for his thoughtlessness, with one of the most scathing rebukes coming from the Simon Wiesenthal Center, an international Jewish human rights group. "This was a shameful act, displaying insensitivity for the victims," read a statement from the organization. "Not just for those soldiers of his own country who gave their lives to defeat Nazism, but to the victims of the Holocaust who were the principal victims of the Nazis."[29]

Harry issued an official apology, which read in part: "I am very sorry if I caused any offense or embarrassment to anyone. It was a poor choice of costume and I apologize."[30] But the backlash continued. Journalist Richard Kay explained, "He simply didn't think. There is a thoughtlessness about many of his actions. He doesn't seem to appreciate yet that what he does actually matters. If it had been one of his friends who'd dressed up in a German uniform, it wouldn't have mattered at all. But it is because it's Prince Harry, it's because he's the third in line to the throne, he

The *Sun's* original headline made its way around the world, causing further public outcry against Harry's poor judgment.

has to be responsible."[31] Even though Harry publicly apologized and many groups worldwide accepted his apology, his lapse in judgment has followed him throughout his adult life.

An Uncertain Future

While many royals before him were trained to become military leaders due to near constant wartime, Prince Harry and Prince William were a new generation of royalty constantly thrust into the limelight and scrutinized by the media. The wave of media attention Harry had received from the point he began at Eton through his gap year called into question Harry's ability to be a functional member of the royal family and whether he had the self-discipline required for a career in the army. Meanwhile, Harry did his best to cope with portrayals of him as a spoiled, out-of-control party prince but admitted, "I'd love to let it wash over me, but I can't—I don't think anyone can. It is hard."[32]

Sir Richard Needham, a British politician who had spent time with the royal family, agreed with Harry. "What a monstrous life those two boys have to live," he commented. "Why can't they live their own lives? It's really, really awful. They are the only people in this country born into something from which they have absolutely no escape and in which they are hounded, absolutely hounded."[33]

Even though Harry's gap year was formative for him, people interpreted his desire to lead a normal life as uncertainty about what his future may hold. Harry, however, was determined to enter the military and fight for his country. Many of his friends and family knew this would be a positive way for Harry to channel his energy.

Prince Harry spent part of his gap year working with cattle and repairing the grounds on a ranch at Tooloombilla Station in Australia.

Chapter **Three**

Ten Years in
the Military

Harry's childhood fascination with the military eventually came to fruition. After participating in Eton College's Combined Cadet Force as cadet officer, receiving the results of his school-leaving examinations, and passing his Regular Commissions Board, Harry was well prepared to begin his military career.

Harry's gap year allowed him to gain valuable work experience and pursue his interest in sports. In September 2003, Harry began a three-month stint as a jackeroo, which is an inexperienced young man who works as an apprentice on a sheep ranch, at Tooloombilla Station, a 400,000-acre (162,000 ha) sheep farm in the Australian outback. In spring 2004, Harry followed in his mother's footsteps and embarked on an eight-week visit to Lesotho, a small, landlocked kingdom surrounded by South Africa, to work with orphaned children whose parents had died from acquired immunodeficiency syndrome (AIDS). In September 2004, Harry spent six weeks training as an assistant development officer with the Rugby Football Union and helping rugby coaches throughout the country teach the game to people of all ages. In November 2004, Harry extended his gap year and spent five weeks working and improving his polo skills on the El Remanso ranch in Argentina. After recovering from a knee injury sustained playing rugby, Harry began what would become a 10-year career in the military with a 44-week training course at the Royal Military Academy Sandhurst in May 2005.

Starting at Sandhurst

The Royal Military Academy Sandhurst, located in Camberley, is where all British army officers undergo training. In order to win a spot in the academy, Harry had to take the Regular Commissions Board (RCB), a four-day assessment that consists of physical tests, written tests, an interview, a planning exercise, and a team competition. The average pass rate of the RCB is about 60 percent.

Prince Charles accompanied Harry to Sandhurst on his first day. They were greeted by several of the academy's leaders. Prince Charles gave him words of encouragement and a playful punch

Harry's life at Sandhurst was unlike anything he had experienced before. While at Eton, a maid cleaned his room. However, at Sandhurst, he was expected to follow the rules and regulations just like all the other cadets.

Held Hostage at Eton

Although his formal training had not yet begun, Harry proved his longtime desire to be a soldier while he was still a student at Eton College. In March 2002, when Harry was just 17 years old, he volunteered to be the hostage as part of Eton's Combined Cadet Force escape and evasion exercise. Five cadets dressed as Taliban soldiers, complete with assault rifles, took Harry hostage in a barn in the town of Boveney. Other cadets were tasked with finding and rescuing him.

Harry's "captors" put a hood over his head and interrogated him for 12 grueling hours. One of the participants in the exercise explained, "They moved him around to disorientate him, forced him to stand leaning on his finger tips against the wall and to kneel. And they shouted at him but he did exactly as he should. He said he was scared and injured to distract them and would only tell them his name, date and place of birth."[1] Despite being tired, humiliated, and at times near tears, Harry repeatedly answered their screamed demands for more information by replying politely, "I'm sorry sir, I cannot answer that question."[2] Harry's "rescuers" were unable to find him, and he was returned to Eton at 5:00 a.m. the following day. This was excellent practice for Harry's future military career in which he might face a similar situation.

1. Quoted in Robert Jobson, *Harry's War*. London, UK: John Blake, 2008, p. 76.

2. Quoted in Mark Saunders, *Prince Harry: The Biography*. London, UK: John Blake, 2002, p. 198.

on the arm before leaving him to start his military training. "I am really excited," Harry said. "I want to get on with it and do the best job I can do."[34] After Harry enrolled and picked up the keys to his room, he was given a red name badge that read "WALES" in white letters. During his training, Harry was referred to as Officer Cadet Wales.

Prince Harry began his 44 weeks of training at Sandhurst with 270 other recruits. Harry was treated just like any other cadet at Sandhurst. He joined 29 other recruits in the Alamein squad. The first five weeks of training were grueling. Cadets had to wake up at dawn and were not allowed to leave the academy. Cadets also were not allowed to have visitors and could not make phone calls.

Sandhurst's reputation for breaking cadets down and building them back up again was expected to break Prince Harry's old habits and help him form new ones as well as bond with his fellow cadets. "Sandhurst brings people down to size," said former army major Charles Heyman. "It's a big reality check and, the further up the pyramid you are, the bigger the shock. It will change him. I think he'll mature quite quickly after forty-four weeks at Sandhurst. They will not care that he's Prince Harry."[35]

Before arriving at Sandhurst, Harry was given a list of supplies he needed, which included his own ironing board. He also needed to have his head neatly shaved. Life at Sandhurst was a huge adjustment for Harry. The cadets had to wake up and be ready for inspection by 5:30 a.m. each day. His bed had to be immaculately made with tight hospital corners. His uniform had to be expertly ironed and precisely folded, and his boots had to be polished until they shone. Daily life for cadets consisted of tasks such as polishing boots, ironing uniforms, intensive drill sessions, and grueling physical exercises. They all went through basic drill, weapons training, and map readings. They spent time in classrooms, on the parade grounds, and outdoors for training. Harry and the other cadets also attended leadership training classes.

Harry lost weight, his feet blistered, and he was shouted at by sergeant majors—just like everyone else in training with him. He said that he was treated "like a piece of dirt" while at

Despite the serious nature of his training, Harry still cracked a smile when he saw his grandmother at his graduation.

Sandhurst but that the experience changed him for the better and helped him grow up. "Nobody's really supposed to love it, it's Sandhurst,"[36] Harry joked.

Toward the end of Harry's time at Sandhurst, he decided that, upon finishing his training, he would like to join an infantry regiment. "I do enjoy running down a ditch full of mud, firing bullets," he confessed. "It's the way I am. I love it."[37] On April 12, 2006, Prince Harry passed out of Sandhurst in a graduation ceremony known as the Sovereign's Parade with 219 fellow officer cadets. During the Sovereign's Parade, the queen inspects the cadets. As she approached Harry, he smiled at her and blushed. The Blues and Royals of the Household Cavalry Regiment, the army's oldest and most senior regiment, commissioned Harry as 2nd lieutenant. Harry was now ready to serve to lead, Sandhurst's motto.

A Target in Iraq

A major part of being in the military is seeing active duty. Harry had formed close bonds with the dozens of men he commanded in his troop and wanted to be with them to lead them if they went into combat. "There's no way I'm going to put myself through Sandhurst and then sit ... back home while my boys are out fighting for their country,"[38] Harry said in 2005. In May 2006, Harry began specialist training to become an armored reconnaissance troop leader. When he completed his training in October 2006, Harry was chomping at the bit to be sent to Iraq to help defend his country.

In February 2007, Harry got his wish. The Ministry of Defense announced that Harry would accompany his regiment to Iraq, where the United Kingdom (UK) had troops stationed since 2003. Cornet Wales, as he was known in the army, would serve as a troop commander and be in charge of several light tank reconnaissance vehicles. His deployment to Iraq would make Harry the first member of the royal family to be sent to a war zone since 1982, when his uncle, Prince Andrew, was sent to the Falkland Islands as a Royal Navy helicopter pilot during the brief war there. Concerns for Harry's safety were immediately raised. Britain's Ministry of Defense feared that, as a royal and a blood relative of the queen, he would be a target for kidnapping or assassination by terrorists. Furthermore, his very presence in a war zone would place those serving with him in extra danger.

The Ministry of Defense's concerns were almost immediately validated. Soon after the announcement of Harry's deployment—which was widely reported in newspapers—Abu Zaid, the commander of an enemy insurgent brigade in Iraq, released a chilling statement, which read, "We are awaiting the arrival of the young, handsome, spoiled prince with bated breath. He will return to his grandmother but without ears."[39] The leader of another insurgent group made it clear that Harry would not be able to hide his identity in Iraq. The army and the Ministry of Defense realized it was very likely Harry would be specifically targeted if he were to go to Iraq. The situation led the media to nickname Harry "the bullet magnet."[40]

The threats on Harry's life and the potential endangerment of his men caused the army to cancel his deployment to Iraq in May 2007. "There have been a number of specific threats— some reported and some not reported—which relate directly to Prince Harry as an individual," said General Richard Dannatt, the head of the British army. "These threats expose not only him but also those around him to a degree of risk that I now deem unacceptable."[41]

Despite understanding and agreeing with the army's decision to cancel his deployment, Harry was absolutely devastated. "I would never want to put someone else's life in danger when they have to sit next to the bullet magnet,"[42] Harry explained. An official statement released on his behalf read: "He fully understands and accepts General Dannatt's difficult decision and remains committed to his Army career. Prince Harry's thoughts are with his troop and the rest of the battle group in Iraq."[43]

Serving in Secret

Harry continued to pursue serving in active duty. In June 2007, Harry met with senior officials in the Ministry of Defense, including Dannatt, to discuss a tour of duty in Afghanistan, where the United Kingdom had stationed troops since 2001. During the meeting, Harry emphasized that he was determined to serve in combat and stated that he would seriously consider leaving the military if he were not allowed to go. Top military officials did not want that to happen, so they came up with a plan for Harry to serve as a battlefield air controller in Afghanistan.

Plans of Harry's previously scheduled deployment had been highly publicized throughout the world. This time, the military was adamant about doing things differently. Dannatt met off the record with newspaper and broadcasting executives and explained that in order for a tour of duty in a war zone to be successful for Harry, the media would have to agree to a voluntary news blackout. The British media executives agreed not to report anything about Harry's deployment, although they could not be responsible for foreign media or the internet. Still, it was a key factor in being able to get Harry covertly into Afghanistan without inviting the same threats that he would be kidnapped or killed by insurgents. Harry was sent to Canadian Forces Base Suffield for three months for training to be a battlefield air controller.

In mid-December 2007, under the utmost secrecy, Harry flew to Helmand Province in southern Afghanistan. In an interview that was not made public until after his deployment ended, Harry said, "No one really knows where I am, and I prefer to keep it that way, for the meantime, until I get back in one piece. Then I can tell them where I was."[44] He was elated to be joining his brothers-in-arms in the Household Cavalry Regiment and do his part in the war on terror. Conditions in Helmand were unforgiving. Nighttime temperatures plunged to well below freezing, the sleeping areas had no heat, and there was almost no running water and very little shelter. Those stationed there, including Harry, could not bathe, shave, or wash their uniforms for days at a time.

The young prince expected and got no special privileges. For example, Christmas fell a few days after his arrival, and Harry received the same extra 10 minutes on his army satellite phone that every other British soldier got for the holiday. David Baxter, a corporal who served in Helmand with Harry, said, "We were initially surprised to see him ... but at the end of the day he is just treated the same as any other officer."[45] While in Helmand, Harry ate army rations and slept on a cot or in a hole dug in the ground just like everyone else. He was proud to be one of the men.

Being just like any other soldier extended to other areas of his deployment as well. Just as there had been concerns over his personal safety if he went into combat, there were concerns about him going out on patrol because of the risk he might be recognized by local insurgents. However, in his camouflage uniform, the third in line to the British throne looked pretty much like all the other soldiers. As Harry put it, "Just walking around,

Just like other soldiers, Harry had duties he had to carry out while deployed in Afghanistan. Here, he can be seen holding a rifle on patrol through the deserted town of Garmsir.

some of the locals or the ANP [Afghan National Police]—they haven't got a clue who I am, they wouldn't know."[46]

Harry, who has been recognized almost everywhere he has ever gone from the time he was a baby, considered his newfound anonymity a welcome change of pace. "It's fantastic," he said. "I'm still a little bit conscious [not to] show my face too much in and around the area. Luckily, there's no civilians around here. ... It's sort of a little no-man's-land."[47] He was careful, however, to keep his face slightly covered whenever he was in more populated areas so that he would not risk being recognized and put himself and his fellow soldiers in danger.

Harry's anonymity even extended to some of the other soldiers serving there. His duties in Helmand included firing a machine gun to repel an enemy attack, patrolling in hostile areas, and calling in air strikes against enemy targets. The pilots he spoke with for hours on the radio every day knew him only by his call name, Widow Six Seven. According to Baxter, "He has always got a rapport with the pilots. I'm sure they would be quite shocked as well if they knew who they were talking to."[48]

Harry's Whereabouts Leaked

On January 7, 2008, just ten weeks into Prince Harry's deployment in Afghanistan, the Australian magazine *New Idea* published information about his tour of duty on its website. However, when the Drudge Report, a U.S.-based website, picked up the story, news of Harry's whereabouts spread throughout the world. Soon after, the British news media began to report the news as well, which angered Dannatt.

Shortly after his cover was blown, Harry was seen as a prime target for the enemy and consequently pulled out of Afghanistan in February 2008 to protect him and his comrades. This was the second time Harry's military career had taken a serious hit, and he was disappointed and frustrated when his tour had to be cut short. However, he was grateful for the time he had spent there and said he wanted to return to the front lines "very, very soon."[49] Harry, who was promoted to lieutenant in April 2008, was awarded an Operational Service Medal for his service in Afghanistan.

On May 5, 2008, the Princess Royal, Queen Elizabeth's daughter Anne, presented Prince Harry with a campaign medal for his service in Afghanistan. About 160 members of the Household Cavalry also received this medal.

Joining the Army Air Corps

Prince Harry decided to continue pursuing his military career in the hopes of serving another tour of duty. In October 2008, he volunteered for selection to be a helicopter pilot with the Army Air Corps. Harry attended "grading," which is a four-week assessment of an applicant's suitability and readiness for further training. In December 2008, Harry got word that he had passed his grading and Pilot's Selection Board interview and would be able to begin his pilot's training in January 2009.

A Humbling Flight Home

On Harry's flight back to England from Afghanistan, several wounded soldiers accompanied him. Two of these soldiers were so seriously injured that they were unconscious during the entire flight. Meeting these wounded servicemen moved him and left a lasting impression on Harry, as he explained:

Those are the heroes. Those were guys who had been blown up by a mine that they had no idea about, serving their country, doing a normal patrol. The bravery of the guys out there was humbling. I wouldn't say I'm a hero. I'm no more a hero than anyone else. If you think about it there are thousands and thousands of troops out there. ... The bravery of the guys out there is just humbling, it's amazing. There were a lot of people in a worse situation than me, that's for sure.[1]

1. Quoted in Robert Jobson, *Harry's War*. London, UK: John Blake, 2008, pp. 219–220.

As a pilot, Harry would have drastically less contact with people on the ground, and he would therefore be less likely to be recognized.

In April 2010, Prince Harry completed the Army Pilots Course. His instructors decided that Harry was well suited to being an Apache or a Lynx pilot. Harry was then allowed to choose which type of helicopter he would prefer to pilot. However, the chain of command had the final decision about which type of aircraft he would pilot. On the day of his graduation from training, Prince Harry was selected to train on the Apache attack helicopter. "It is a huge honour to have the chance to train on the Apache, which is an awesome helicopter,"[50] Harry said.

In April 2011, Prince Harry was promoted to the rank of captain. At that time, he was also awarded his Apache badge from the officer in command of his squadron to mark his completion of an eight-month Apache training course. In October 2011, Prince Harry visited the United States to complete his Apache training. This training was a two-month exercise, known as Exercise

In a graduation ceremony on May 7, 2010, Prince Charles presented Prince Harry with his provisional wings. Prince Charles is the colonel-in-chief of the Army Air Corps.

Crimson Eagle. The exercise included environmental training, in which students had to handle their aircraft in mountain and desert conditions, and judgmental training, in which students had to use weapon systems in different situations. One of the final phases of Exercise Crimson Eagle involved a realistic live firing scenario. At the end of the course, Harry was awarded the prize for best copilot gunner.

In February 2012, after 18 months of intensive training to learn to fly and fight in the Apache attack helicopter, Prince Harry qualified as a copilot gunner and became a fully operational Apache pilot. He was posted to 3 Regiment Army Air Corps, which is part of 16 Air Assault Brigade. In this position, Prince Harry was able to gain further flying experience and practice operating the aircraft in different kinds of exercises.

Captain Harry Wales was again deployed to Afghanistan in September 2012. For this deployment, there was no media blackout. He was stationed in Camp Bastion in Helmand province and provided helicopter support to foreign and Afghan forces there until January 2013. In 2014, he took the position of staff officer at HQ London District. In this role, he helped plan major ceremonial events involving the army, such as Trooping the Colour, which is a traditional military parade that honors the birthday of the monarch. Since his time in the military, Prince Harry has devoted a large part of his life to supporting Britain's servicemen and women.

Chapter **Four**

Humanitarian Harry

Throughout Prince Harry's adult life, he has been committed to participating in charitable activities and donating to causes in which he strongly believes. Today, Prince Harry donates to and is the patron of a number of charities. Some of the causes closest to Harry's heart are those that support Britain's servicemen and women and those that support children living with human immunodeficiency virus (HIV), which is the incurable virus that causes AIDS, and AIDS. Part of Harry's role as a member of the royal family is carrying out duties to support the queen. His charitable work and official tours in the UK and overseas give him a platform to promote his humanitarian efforts.

Continuing Diana's Work

Princess Diana earned the nickname the "People's Princess" for her compassion and dedication to not only the people of Britain but people everywhere. Harry has made it clear that he intends to carry on Diana's legacy of helping others less fortunate than he is. His mother was well known for her humanitarian efforts, including her work to help the underprivileged, the poor, and the sick, particularly those afflicted with HIV/AIDS. She related to people in a way that no member of British royalty had ever done before. She was photographed shaking hands with AIDS patients, which helped alleviate the formerly widespread fear that AIDS was spread by physical touch and removed some of the social stigma of AIDS. She involved both her boys in her humanitarian efforts from the time they were little. Diana wanted to make sure her sons knew about the harsh realities of life outside the palace walls.

Diana often discussed the plight of the needy with Harry and William in family talks after dinner. She wanted them to grow up understanding that not everyone in the world shared their wealth and privilege, and as a result, both boys understood that disadvantaged people existed all over the world. From the time they were young, Harry's and William's teachers noted their good

Princess Diana visited AIDS wards throughout the United Kingdom and abroad to help raise awareness for the disease. She was the patron of the National AIDS Trust.

manners and their consideration for others, traits Diana worked hard to instill in them.

Due in large part to his mother's efforts, Harry showed an early commitment to philanthropic causes. When he was eight years old, he overheard his mother talking with members of the British Red Cross about the difficulties faced by people in war-torn Sarajevo. He immediately volunteered to go with an aid convoy that was headed to the former Yugoslavia. Unfortunately, Charles and Diana informed him that would not be possible.

Diana remains one of Prince Harry's biggest role models to this day. "I always think of my mother in everything I do," he said. "I hope she would be proud of my work."[51] Harry's first foray into

Sending Aid to Tsunami Victims

In response to reports of children orphaned by tsunamis throughout the Indian Ocean in December 2004, Princes Harry and William volunteered in a warehouse preparing and loading hygiene packs, which included essential toiletries such as soap, toothbrushes, and toothpaste, for the Red Cross. The Red Cross sent the packs to the island nation of the Maldives, where more than 20,000 people were displaced or temporarily relocated due to the tsunami. "We just wanted to be hands on," Harry said. "We didn't want to sit back."[1]

More than 230,000 people in 14 countries perished in what was one of the deadliest natural disasters in history. There was an outpouring of international aid and support for the survivors, which included 10 million people who were homeless or displaced.

1. Quoted in BBC, "Princes Help Prepare Tsunami Aid," January 7, 2005. news.bbc.co.uk/2/hi/uk_news/4154687.stm.

supporting charitable causes was during his gap year, during which he visited Lesotho in southern Africa.

Helping in Lesotho

As part of Harry's gap year, he went on a two-month working trip to Lesotho in southern Africa. Lesotho had been plagued by AIDS, poverty, and drought for many years. Prince Harry spent time at an orphanage about 62 miles (100 km) from the capital city of Maseru. All of the children at the orphanage had lost both parents to AIDS. At the time of Harry's visit, more than one-third of the country's population was HIV positive. One of Harry's goals was to increase British aid in Lesotho. The press was invited to the orphanage for a one-day photo call, during which Harry was photographed and filmed doing basic manual labor, playing with the orphans, and cradling tiny children in his arms.

Harry was so moved by the AIDS orphans he met that he produced *The Forgotten Kingdom: Prince Harry in Lesotho*. The 35-minute documentary shows footage of Harry interacting with children at the orphanage and talking to people in the village who had HIV or AIDS. Harry's natural affinity with children was evident as he played with them, spoke to them, and walked hand-in-hand with them. During his time in Lesotho, Harry formed bonds with many children. One of the things he liked most about his interactions with the children was they did not know who he was and they treated him like a normal person.

Harry's time in Lesotho inspired him. In the documentary he said, "We want to do more, and we can."[52] And he did. In 2006, he and Prince Seeiso, the younger brother of the king of Lesotho, cofounded Sentebale, which means "forget me not" in Sesotho, the language spoken in Lesotho. The name Sentebale was chosen as a tribute to both princes' late mothers' work with those affected by AIDS and poverty and also as a way to prevent the situation in Lesotho from being forgotten. Sentebale helps impoverished children get care, support, and education so they can lead happy and healthy lives. "I really feel that by doing this I can follow in my mother's footsteps and keep her legacy alive,"[53] Harry explained.

Since 2004, Harry has traveled to Lesotho several times, helping

While at Mants'ase Children's Home in Mohale's Hoek, Lesotho, Prince Harry befriended and formed a close bond with a young boy named Mutsu (pictured here). In May 2018, Prince Harry flew Mutsu to the United Kingdom for his wedding.

build orphanages, a school for the blind, and a refuge for young mothers. "Harry wants to make a difference," William explained, "and I've seen it with Sentebale. ... Out here, he is the star, to be honest. They love him out here, for what Sentebale has become."[54] Today, everywhere Harry travels, he participates in activities to help raise funds for Sentebale, such as concerts, charity rallies, and polo matches. In 2016, Prince Harry returned to Lesotho—a decade after cofounding the charity. In a TV documentary produced to commemorate the event, Harry highlighted Sentebale's plans to expand into five sub-Saharan African countries by 2020. This expansion would help young adults cope with living with HIV.

Teaming Up with William

Prince Harry is a patron or president of many charities and organizations throughout the world. In April 2006, Harry and William created the Charities Forum to help foster collaboration among their many charitable interests. The forum began with the princes' earlier patronages—Centrepoint, the Football Association, Tusk Trust, and Sentebale—and has grown to involve more than 30 organizations. Included in these are Dolen Cymru, MapAction, WellChild, the Khumbu Challenge 2009, and the Henry van Straubenzee Memorial Fund.

The charities in the forum support the princes' main areas of interest, including supporting members of the armed forces and their families, helping children and young people, and supporting environmentalism. The different member charities also have the opportunity to work together on projects, which would not have been possible without the forum.

In September 2009, Harry and William launched the Royal Foundation to further their humanitarian efforts. It became fully operational in 2011 when Kate Middleton, the Duchess of Cambridge, joined as a principal patron. The main themes of the foundation are mental health, wildlife and conservation, young people, and the armed forces community. "We are both massively excited at the prospect of being able to help in whatever way we can, where we can," Harry said. "If we can use our position to do this, we are ready to."[55] One of the goals of the foundation is to

The Duke of Sussex is a patron of WellChild, a charity that makes it possible for children and young people with health needs to be cared for at home instead of in the hospital. He and the Duchess of Sussex are shown here at a WellChild event.

develop projects and then allow them to become self-sustaining. For example, the Invictus Games was developed by the foundation but now runs independently. Upon her marriage to Prince Harry, the Duchess of Sussex became the fourth principal patron.

Heads Together

Mental health is a very important issue to Prince Harry. In May 2016, Prince Harry and the Duke and Duchess of Cambridge—William and Kate—partnered to start the Heads Together mental health campaign and lead a coalition of eight mental health charity partners to destigmatize talking about mental health and raise funds for

Prince William, Prince Harry, and Kate Middleton work with the Heads Together campaign. Prince Harry and Kate Middleton have a strong relationship. She has been like a sister to him.

innovative mental health services. The campaign aims to open up the conversation about mental health and help those struggling seek help without fear of being judged. The Heads Together campaign is also supported by the Royal Foundation.

Heads Together was chosen as the 2017 Virgin Money London Marathon Charity of the Year. This allowed the campaign to raise funds for its charity partners and served as the catalyst for countless conversations about mental health. As the United Kingdom's premier charity sports event, the London Marathon was a very effective way for Heads Together to spread its message.

In a 2017 interview, Prince Harry opened up about his mental health struggles in the wake of his mother's death. For nearly 20 years, Harry kept his grief to himself until he could not take it anymore. He sought counseling after two years of particularly bad anxiety and anger. Prince Harry spoke to Bryony Gordon on the first episode of her podcast "Mad World," stating, "I have probably been very close to a complete breakdown on numerous occasions when all sorts of grief and sort of lies and misconceptions and everything are coming to you from every angle."[56] However, Harry has said that a combination of counseling and letting out aggression through boxing has helped him immensely. He encourages people to talk about their mental health and seek help when the timing is right.

Harry's Royal Duties

Harry undertakes official royal engagements in the United Kingdom and overseas in support of the queen in addition to his charitable activities. His royal duties include making public appearances and attending photo shoots and interviews. When Harry turned 21 years old in 2005, he joined his grandfather, father, and brother, as well as his uncle, Prince Andrew, as a counsellor of state, which means that he is able to stand in for the queen during certain state functions, such as attending meetings or signing documents. He also began making official royal visits of his own.

Harry's first official royal visit on behalf of the queen took place in March 2012. He visited Belize, the Bahamas, and Jamaica as part of the queen's diamond jubilee celebrations, which commemorated the 60th anniversary of her coronation. These three countries are part of the Commonwealth of Nations (nations that have Queen Elizabeth as their monarch and head of state). "Prince Harry is really bouncing about the visit," said Jamie Lowther-Pinkerton, Harry's private secretary, in a statement announcing the visit. "The Prince is hugely looking forward to representing the Queen and he will bring his own brand of enthusiasm and energy to every event."[57]

During his weeklong tour, Harry kept busy with official activities, which included meeting with government officials, visiting with schoolchildren, talking with military personnel, taking part in military exercises, and attending services to mark the jubilee. Especially close to Harry's heart was his visit to Bustamante

What Does the Monarch Do?

The king or queen of the United Kingdom is the constitutional monarch of 16 sovereign states known as the Commonwealth realms, which include Canada, Australia, and New Zealand, as well as the head of 53 nations that make up the Commonwealth of Nations. In addition, the British monarch is the head of the Church of England and appoints bishops and arch-bishops. The monarch holds very little political power—with one notable exception. The monarch is the head of all of Britain's armed forces and is the only person in the nation with the power to declare war.

The monarch carries out many important tasks on behalf of the nation. These include making official vis-its abroad, as well as welcoming other world leaders who visit the United Kingdom. Even when not abroad, the monarch still spends a great deal of time travel-ing, visiting schools, hospitals, factories, and various organizations. Whether traveling or at home, the mon-arch carries out daily government duties that include reading and signing documents and reports from gov-ernment officials. Handling the responsibilities of the British monarchy is a full-time job, one that dictates how the king or queen spends each day of his or her reign—and also a lifetime job that can only be "quit" by abdication or death.

Hospital for Children in Kingston, Jamaica. He toured several wards and play areas at the hospital, then unveiled a plaque at the entrance in honor of the queen.

After his tour of Belize, the Bahamas, and Jamaica, Harry traveled to Brazil on behalf of the British government. Part

Queen Elizabeth II is the longest reigning monarch in British history. She has traveled more widely than any other monarch and has been a steadfast figure in times of radical change in the United Kingdom and the Commonwealth.

of the purpose of his visit was to promote British culture and exports and to support the launch of the GREAT campaign, which fosters links between Britain and Brazil. To kick off the campaign, he traveled by cable car to a plateau at the base of Rio de Janeiro's Sugarloaf Mountain, where he delivered his

Harry's royal duties include attending military events. On November 8, 2018, he attended the opening of the Field of Remembrance at Westminster Abbey.

first speech in Brazil. He also visited the world-famous Cristo Redentor (Christ the Redeemer) statue above Rio de Janeiro. During his three-day tour of Brazil, Harry also participated in several events to help promote the 2012 Olympic Games in London.

While in Brazil, Harry also engaged in activities that supported his own charitable activities and interests. He took part in the

Sentebale Polo Cup in São Paolo, which aimed to raise money and awareness for the charity's activities to help orphans and vulnerable children in Lesotho. Harry played for the Sentebale team and also delivered a speech at a lunch after the match. After the polo cup, which marked the end of Harry's official visit, he made a private journey to the interior of Brazil in order to learn more about conservation and the natural world, a personal interest of his.

Over the years, Harry's dedication to helping others has grown and diversified. He is committed to furthering his mother's legacy and forging his own path to support causes close to his heart. His royal duties also allow him to branch out and utilize his skills to unite the Commonwealth.

Chapter **Five**

Harry Today

While Harry's youth was characterized by dangerous stunts and his military career, today, Prince Harry performs royal duties as the Duke of Sussex. He still enjoys many of the things he did when he was younger, including playing sports and contributing to philanthropic efforts. Harry also continues to have a close bond with his family, especially his father and brother.

Prince Harry's confidence as a royal was boosted by serving dutifully in the British army and devoting a great deal of his time to humanitarian causes and charities. In recent years, Prince Harry has gone on a number of diplomatic trips and taken on new positions with different government organizations and within the Commonwealth. Harry's future as an important member of the royal family is rooted in his commitment to listening to people's needs and addressing some of the world's most pressing issues.

Prince Harry's Closest Friends

Many of Prince Harry's closest friends have been a part of his life since childhood. His friends are sources of inspiration and advice in all areas of life. As a result of being friends with

Prince Harry, a number of his friends have been thrust into the limelight. Harry has admitted that friends of his and William's get hounded by photographers, just as they do. "It's just as hard for our friends as it is for us," Harry said. "Our friends have to put up with a lot when it comes to us."[58]

Tom "Skippy" Inskip is one of Harry's closest friends. The two men met at Eton College and have been fixtures in each other's lives since then. Skippy's marriage to Lara Hughes-Young in Jamaica was one of the first times Harry and Meghan Markle were seen together as a couple.

Thomas van Straubenzee is a close friend of many of the younger generation of British royalty. Thomas is the older brother of one of Harry's closest friends at Ludgrove, Henry van Straubenzee. In 2002, when he was just 19 years old, Henry was killed when the car in which he was riding crashed into a tree. Henry's death was devastating for Harry, who had lost his mother in a tragic car crash only five years earlier. Today, Prince Harry, Thomas, and Prince William are patrons of the Henry van Straubenzee Memorial Fund, which is dedicated to improving education for the children of Uganda. Thomas is also the godfather of Princess Charlotte.

Hugh Grosvenor, the Duke of Westminster, is very close with the royal family. He is part of one of Britain's most influential families and is one of the richest men in the world. He is one of Prince George's godfathers.

Jake Warren, one of Princess Diana's godsons, is another close friend of Prince Harry's. The two boys grew up together and attended Ludgrove preparatory school and Eton College together. They are often seen together at royal events.

Guy Pelly has been friends with Prince William and Prince Harry for many years. In 2013, Pelly was named one of Prince George's godfathers. In 2014, the princes went to the United States to attend Pelly's marriage to Lizzy Wilson. Pelly's mother, Lady Carolyn Herbert, was a close friend of Princess Diana's.

A number of Prince Harry's friends' children were in his wedding. Zalie Warren (back row, right), Jake Warren's daughter, was Meghan's youngest bridesmaid at just two years old.

Harry and Chelsy

Although Harry was often dubbed a ladies' man in his younger years, his relationship with Zimbabwean Chelsy Davy was one of his first serious romantic relationships and one of the most highly publicized. Harry first met Chelsy while she was a student at Cheltenham Ladies' College, near Highgrove House. After graduating from Cheltenham, she attended the University of Cape Town in South Africa. When Harry stopped for a visit in Cape Town on his way to Lesotho during his gap year, the two met up and fell in love. A friend of Harry's reported that while sitting next to the fire on a camping trip in Botswana, Harry "couldn't stop talking about her."[59] William told friends that Harry was "madly in love"[60] with Chelsy. Like Harry, she loved the outdoors and adored animals. In an interview early in their relationship, Harry described her as "very special" and "amazing."[61]

Prince Harry and Chelsy Davy had an on again/off again relationship. Chelsy was present at many of the most significant events of Harry's life during this time. She and Kate Middleton watched polo matches from the sidelines. She sat

A Perfect Gentleman

In October 2011, Harry arrived in California for a two-month stay for military helicopter training. One night, Harry and his friends were watching an England rugby match on TV at the Andaz Hotel's rooftop pool in San Diego. A man picked up 23-year-old Lindsay Swagerty, an office worker who was at the rooftop bar with her friend, and jumped into the pool with her fully clothed— "high heels and all,"[1] Swagerty said. Even though it was all in good fun, Harry came to her aid. He offered her his towel, wrapping it around her to keep her warm. Swagerty was delighted to meet the prince and even more delighted by his gentlemanly gesture. She kept his towel as a souvenir, and the following night, she and several of her friends met him and his friends at the hotel again for drinks. "He is probably the most charming man I'll ever meet,"[2] Swagerty said.

1. Quoted in Simon Perry and Stephen M. Silverman, "Prince Harry Comes to the Rescue at Pool Party," *People*, October 12, 2011. people.com/royals/prince-harry-hero-of-the-rooftop-bar-pool.

2. Quoted in Simon Perry and Stephen M. Silverman, "Prince Harry Comes to the Rescue at Pool Party."

in the front row with Harry during the Concert for Diana in 2007. In May 2008, Chelsy attended the ceremony in which Prince Harry received his Operational Service Medal for his service in Afghanistan. Later that month, she attended the wedding of Harry's cousin Peter Phillips to Autumn Kelly. In early 2009, Prince Harry and Chelsy broke up. However, they got back together at the end of the year. In May 2010, Chelsy attended Prince Harry's graduation ceremony from an advanced helicopter-training course in which Harry was awarded his provisional wings from Prince Charles. Later that month, Harry and Chelsy broke up again. In 2011, she attended the wedding of Prince William and Kate Middleton, but she said she would not marry Prince Harry because a life in the spotlight was not the type of life she envisioned for herself. Harry's and Chelsy's lives still crossed paths on more than one occasion. She was a bridesmaid in the wedding of Harry's friend Thomas van Straubenzee to Melissa Percy. She was also invited to the ceremony portion of Prince Harry's wedding to Meghan Markle.

After Harry and Chelsy split for good, there were several rumors concerning his love life. One of these was that he was involved with Pippa Middleton, Kate Middleton's younger sister. Harry and Pippa had met each other several times for tea after William and Kate's wedding and had talked on the telephone on numerous occasions. Harry even ended his best man's speech at William and Kate's wedding by suggesting that Pippa should call him sometime. He was only joking around, though, and he and Pippa were only friends. Harry laughed off any suggestion that the two of them were anything more than friends. "Pippa? … No," Harry told a reporter in June 2011. "I am not seeing anyone at the moment. I'm 100 per cent single."[62]

In the summer of 2012, Princess Eugenie, Prince Harry's cousin, introduced Harry to actress and model Cressida Bonas. The two dated for two years before splitting amicably. Like his relationship with Chelsy Davy, Harry's relationship with Cressida Bonas allegedly came to an end due to how much attention she was getting from the media as a result of dating a royal. She also attended Prince Harry's wedding ceremony.

As a good friend of Princess Eugenie's (left), Cressida Bonas (right) has attended many royal events, including the wedding of Lady Natasha Rufus Isaacs and Rupert Finch at the Church of St. John the Baptist on June 8, 2013, in Cirencester, England.

Royal Weddings Galore

On April 9, 2005, Prince Charles and Camilla Parker Bowles were married in a civil ceremony at Windsor Guildhall and a service of blessing at St. George's Chapel at Windsor Castle. After they were married, Camilla took the name Her Royal Highness the Duchess of Cornwall. Prince William served as one of the couple's witnesses, and all of their children were there to support them. Prince Charles and Camilla had been in love for many years before getting married. Harry and William learned as kids about the emotional anguish their father's affair with Camilla had caused their mother. By 2005, however, they both had met and gotten to know Camilla, and they were openly supportive of their father's second marriage. A longtime friend of both princes said, "William and Harry always wanted their father to be happy, and by this time they were so used to Camilla being there, they didn't feel that they were betraying their mother any longer."[63]

On April 29, 2011, Prince William married Catherine (Kate) Middleton at Westminster Abbey in London. William proposed to Kate with his mother's sapphire and diamond ring while on vacation in Kenya on October 20, 2010. Clarence House announced their engagement on November 16, 2010. William and Kate met at St. Andrews University in Fife, Scotland, in 2001 and began dating in 2003. Millions of people around the world watched and listened to this momentous royal wedding. After their wedding, William and Kate became the Duke and Duchess of Cambridge. Harry served as William's best man and also helped plan the wedding. He was delighted that William had proposed to Kate. "I've always wanted a sister and now I've got one,"[64] he said.

Prince Harry and American actress Meghan Markle began dating in July 2016 after they met through mutual friends in London. In November 2016, Prince Harry confirmed suspicions that he was dating Meghan Markle in a statement from Kensington Palace, which means it is an official royal statement, requesting that media cease its abuse and harassment of Meghan, her family, and her friends. The couple made their first public appearance at an official royal engagement at the opening ceremony of the Invictus Games in Toronto, Canada, in September 2017. On November 27, 2017, Clarence House announced Prince Harry's engagement to Meghan. Harry proposed to Meghan earlier in November at his cottage while roasting chicken. It was an instant "yes" from Meghan. Her engagement ring is yellow gold and has two diamonds from Princess Diana's jewelry collection, and Prince Harry sourced the center diamond from Botswana. Prince Harry and Meghan Markle were married on May 19, 2018, at St. George's Chapel at Windsor Castle. Upon being married, their titles changed to the Duke and Duchess of Sussex. Prince William served as Prince Harry's best man. Meghan did not have a maid of honor. Like the wedding of

Prince Harry was given special permission from Queen Elizabeth to keep his beard for his wedding day. Normally, when wearing an army uniform, soldiers must be clean-shaven.

Prince William and Kate Middleton, millions of people around the world tuned in to Prince Harry and Meghan Markle's wedding.

On October 12, 2018, Princess Eugenie, the queen's grand-daughter and the second daughter of Prince Andrew and Sarah, Duchess of York, married Jack Brooksbank at St. George's Chapel at Windsor Castle. The queen held a reception for the newlyweds and their guests at Windsor Castle. The Duke and Duchess of Sussex, the Duke and Duchess of Cambridge, and many other members of the royal family attended Princess Eugenie's wedding.

Best Friends Forever

Prince Harry and Prince William continue to be best friends. Although their schedules are full of royal duties and philanthropic efforts, they still talk to each other almost every day. Over the years, Harry has become known as more of the playful brother while William has become known as the responsible family man. The princes still enjoy a bit of healthy competition in the sports arena. They have competed against each other in polo matches, have run against each other for charity, and have even ridden motorcycles for charity. They've shared so many experiences throughout their lives, including their time in the military, that their bond is unbreakable.

William and Harry often tease each other, jokingly put each other down, and laugh about it. For example, William sometimes affectionately calls Harry "Ginger," a reference to Harry's reddish hair—and Harry counters by teasing his brother about going bald. During one interview, Harry joked that his older brother was so lazy that he was still crawling at age six. When the

Prince Harry raced against the Duke and Duchess of Cambridge for Team Heads Together at a London Marathon training day at Queen Elizabeth Olympic Park on February 5, 2017, in London.

interviewer described William was dutiful, Harry asked, "Was that 'dutiful' or 'beautiful'?" It was all in good fun, of course. The brothers are just as likely to compliment one another as they are to tease. For example, when pressed later in the same interview to describe his brother, Harry replied earnestly, "You know, he works very hard. He's definitely the more intelligent one of the two of us."[65]

The princes understand and support one another in everything each undertakes and through all of life's ups and downs. Harry feels like his brother is the one person he can talk to about anything. They have always shared a deep bond, and this has only increased since their mother's death. "He is the one person on this earth who I can actually really... we can talk about anything," Harry said. "We understand each other and we give each other support. If I find myself in really hard times, then at least I can turn to him, and vice versa."[66]

However, now that both princes have families of their own, they have split their formerly shared Kensington Palace household—Prince William will continue living at Kensington Palace while Prince Harry and Meghan Markle will live at Frogmore Cottage on the Windsor estate. While some may think this will shatter the brothers' bond, it is necessary for their lives to progress. William's potential role as the king of England is at the forefront of his mind. Harry can exercise his freedom a bit more because he is further down in the line of succession to the throne. William and Harry remain close despite the separation of the houses of Cambridge and Sussex.

Remembering Diana

Both Prince Harry and Prince William had a close bond with their mother. They wanted to find a way to remember her in a way she would have been proud of. On July 1, 2007, Prince William and Prince Harry hosted a benefit concert to mark the 10th anniversary of Princess Diana's death. The concert, which was held on what would have been her 46th birthday, raised an estimated $10 million, which was split between Diana's charities and charities William and Harry supported. Held at the newly

Prince William and Prince Harry spoke to the audience at the Concert for Diana. They reminded concertgoers why they decided to host the concert: their mother's love of music and dancing, her charities, and her family and friends.

built Wembley Stadium in London, the concert was attended by more than 60 thousand people, with another 500 million in 140 countries around the world watching on TV.

The star-studded concert included performances by Rod Stewart, Duran Duran, and Kanye West, among many others, as well as a tribute by Andrew Lloyd Webber prepared especially for the occasion. Perhaps the most notable performance was that of Elton John, who was one of Diana's closest friends and who had sung at her funeral.

Harry's role in organizing and hosting the concert showed that he was capable of handling the adult responsibilities that come along with his royal status and his place in line to succeed the throne. This more mature side was further demonstrated during the memorial service held at Guards' Chapel, Wellington Barracks, central London, on August 31 to mark the 10th anniversary of Diana's death. Harry and William organized the service with the help of Diana's siblings.

Prince William read a passage from the Bible, but moments later, it was Harry who delivered an emotional tribute to their mother. Harry stepped proudly before the congregation of almost 500 people—including Queen Elizabeth, Prince Philip,

Always Thinking of Diana

In 2007, Matt Lauer interviewed Prince Harry and Prince William on the eve of the celebrations to honor Diana's 46th birthday and the 10th anniversary of her death. During the interview, Harry and William spoke candidly about missing their mother and said that the 10 years since her passing had gone by very slowly. "It's weird because I think when she passed away there was never that time, there was never that sort of lull. There was never that sort of peace and quiet for any of us due to the fact that her face was always splattered on the paper the whole time,"[1] Harry said. Both princes said they are always thinking about Diana and had only recently been able to escape the seemingly incessant barrage of media coverage concerning her death. They acknowledged that the media might never stop being fascinated with her life and death. William and Harry used the celebrations as a way to take control of how the media would portray her and also to honor their mother.

1. Quoted in Matt Lauer, "In Honor of Diana," MSNBC.com, June 27, 2007. www.msnbc.msn. com/id/19190534.

Prince Charles, and the new prime minister, Gordon Brown—and a global TV audience of millions. Tall, handsome, and dynamic, Harry spoke eloquently and with a mature poise that surprised many. In the speech he and William had written together, Harry described their mother in the following words: "She was our guardian, friend and protector. She never once allowed her unfaltering love for us to go unspoken or undemonstrated. She will always be remembered for her amazing public work. But behind the media glare, to us, just two loving children, she was quite simply the best mother in the world."[67] The world saw that Harry had grown from the grief-stricken little figure walking solemnly behind Diana's casket into a confident and well-spoken young man.

One of the most influential ways Harry remembers Diana is his continued contributions to charities and participating in humanitarian activities. One of Harry's biggest desires is for people to focus on all the good work Diana did in her short lifetime, such as raising awareness of HIV/AIDS and advocating for an international ban on land mines. "I think people will always have a fascination about her,"[68] Harry said. He wants people to remember Diana for the right reasons—and not for any of the many tabloid stories that were written about her. "It still upsets me now, the fact that we didn't have much of a chance as children to sort of spend time with her," he once said. "But the time we did spend with her was amazing and as a mother, as anybody would say about their mother, [she was] just amazing."[69]

Harry's Daily Life

Harry is a sensitive and charming man. Like their mother, both Harry and William are able to connect with many of the people they speak to. They rarely ever let on to the unimaginable pressures they face as royalty. Harry still likes to live his life as normally as possible—while still carrying out his royal duties. Although he is a member of a royal family and has grown up with privilege, Harry shares many of the same interests as other men his age. He enjoys watching and playing polo and rugby.

In his younger years, Harry enjoyed going dancing and could

sometimes be found partying in nightclubs, wearing jeans and a collared shirt and surrounded by his royal bodyguards and the constant stream of young women who hoped to catch his eye. For many years, Prince Harry smoked cigarettes, a habit he continued even after entering the army. However, Meghan Markle convinced him to quit smoking in an effort to not only get healthy but also to help start a family.

Harry is still very athletic and enjoys all the same sports he did when he was younger. He also likes hunting and rides with the Beaufort Hunt, a fox-hunting group, as do Prince Charles and the Duke of Cambridge—although since 2005, when fox hunting became illegal in England, they no longer shoot on the hunts. Harry still often outperforms his big brother in polo, skiing, and virtually every other sport. Harry and William are both very competitive and will try to best each other—even if they are on the same team. According to Richard Kay, a columnist for the British tabloid the *Daily Mail*, "[Harry is] a great sportsman, fearless skier, very brave on a polo pony, and again, on a horse chasing after foxes and hounds. He is actually better than William in most sports."[70]

Today, when Harry is not traveling around the world for charity or as part of his royal duties, he and the Duchess of Sussex live at Frogmore Cottage, a two-story 17th century cottage that overlooks Frogmore House on the Windsor Castle estate. Before Prince Harry and Meghan Markle were married, they lived in Nottingham Cottage, a snug two-bedroom cottage on the Kensington Palace estate. Shortly after their wedding, the Duke and Duchess moved into Apartment 1, a 21-room dwelling in the main palace building, formerly occupied by the Duke and Duchess of Gloucester. The Duke and Duchess of Cambridge and their three children live in Apartment 1A, a 20-room dwelling overlooking Hyde Park. Princess Eugenie and Jack Brooksbank live in Ivy Cottage, near Harry and Meghan's former residence at Nottingham Cottage.

One of Harry's goals is to live as normal a life as possible. As sixth in the line of succession to the throne, Harry has been afforded more normalcy than William has. However, he must still perform royal duties as they arise. In an exclusive interview

Other royals living on the Kensington Palace estate include the Duke and Duchess of Kent and Prince and Princess Michael of Kent.

with *Newsweek* in June 2017, Harry said, "We are involved in modernizing the British monarchy. We are not doing this for ourselves but for the greater good of the people… Is there any one of the royal family who wants to be king or queen? I don't think so, but we will carry out our duties at the right time."[71] Harry credits his mother with instilling in him a need to prioritize leading as normal a life as possible. He said, "I do my own shopping. Sometimes, when I come away from the meat counter at my local supermarket, I worry someone will snap me with their phone. But I am determined to have a relatively normal life, and if I am lucky enough to have children, they can have one too. Even if I was king, I would do my own shopping."[72]

Harry, just like William and the other members of the royal family, is very wealthy. His net worth is estimated to be between $25 million and $40 million. Diana's mother, Frances Shand Kydd, left them roughly one-fourth of her $4 million estate when she died in 2004, and Diana left them roughly $10.5 million each. In addition, each has inherited millions in assets as members of the royal family. Like his brother, Harry's inheritance was held in trust until he turned 25. At that point, he was allowed to spend the income generated by his portion of the estate, which was approximately $500,000 a year. Prince Harry also receives an annual seven-figure allowance from Prince Charles. During his 10 years of service in the British Royal Air Force, Harry earned about $50,000 a year. When he turned 30 in 2014, he gained access to his entire inheritance. Upon his marriage to Meghan Markle, whose net worth is estimated at some $5 million, their combined net worth rose to over $30 million. Although he is wealthy, Harry prefers to save and invest his money, rather than spending it frivolously.

The Future King?

While it is technically possible for Prince Harry to become the king of England, it is very unlikely. As sixth in the line of succession to the throne, Prince Charles, Prince William, Prince George, Princess Charlotte, and Prince Louis would need to either die or abdicate. It is not unheard of for a king to abdicate, or step aside—most famously in 1936, when King Edward VIII of England gave up the throne so he could marry twice-divorced Wallis Simpson, leaving his younger brother, George VI, to take his place as king. This is not only a part of history, but also a part of Harry and William's family tree; had Edward not abdicated, Elizabeth would not have eventually become queen and her grandson William would not currently be second in line to the throne. William long ago accepted his fate and is ready to embrace his role as king when the time comes. In the past, Harry has been asked if he worried about William abdicating and leaving him with the responsibility of being king. "He assures me that he's not going to do that," Harry said, laughing nervously, but added, "I've had dreams."[73] However, now that William has had children, this is no longer a real concern for Harry.

In April 2018, Queen Elizabeth II passed off her duties as the head of the Commonwealth of Nations, an international organization of 53 member states, to Prince Charles with the permission of Commonwealth heads. Harry—and Prince William—

expressed interest in taking on this role, but the younger generation of royals is not favored to take over the most important Commonwealth duties at this time.

Around the same time as his father's appointment as head of the Commonwealth of Nations, Queen Elizabeth II appointed Prince Harry a Commonwealth youth ambassador. In this role, his highest-profile role to date, Harry, along with Meghan Markle, works to encourage young people to use the Commonwealth as a network and to listen to their needs. Buckingham Palace has stated that more than 60 percent of the Commonwealth's population of 2.4 billion people is under 30 years old. This gives Prince Harry and Meghan Markle quite a large audience to create positive change and further modernize the monarchy in the years to come.

What's Next for the Duke and Duchess of Sussex?

On October 15, 2018, a tweet from Kensington Palace announced that the Duke and Duchess of Sussex were expecting a child in spring 2019. The tweet came just after the couple arrived in Australia for a 16-day tour of Australia, New Zealand, Tonga, and Fiji—their first royal tour as Duke and Duchess—and just after Princess Eugenie's wedding to Jack Brooksbank. The Duke and Duchess's child will be seventh in line to the throne. The child will be referred to as "lord" or "lady" as is customary of children of dukes.

In recent years, Harry has taken on a number of important positions, including president of African Parks, a patron of Walk of America, and president of the Queen's Commonwealth Trust, and in 2018, he was selected as one of *TIME* magazine's 100 Most Influential People in the World. He also launched a global coalition called MenStar with Elton John to focus on treating HIV infections in men.

The Duke of Sussex continues his work with the Invictus Games, which he created in 2014, the HALO Trust, the London Marathon Charitable Trust, and Walking with the Wounded.

As part of their royal duties, the Duke and Duchess of Sussex tour countries of the Commonwealth on behalf of the monarchy.

His dedication to charitable causes reflects his mother's passion for helping those in need. In the years to come, the Duke and Duchess will likely continue to use their elevated status to create positive change in the world. Together, the Duke and Duchess continue to shape the monarchy's identity as a modern entity.

Notes

Introduction: Sixth in Line

1. ITN (Independent Television News), *The Forgotten Kingdom: Prince Harry in Lesotho*. Television Documentary. www.youtube.com/watch?v=ydKOMzknMCk.

2. ITN (Independent Television News), *The Forgotten Kingdom: Prince Harry in Lesotho*.

3. ITN (Independent Television News), *The Forgotten Kingdom: Prince Harry in Lesotho*.

Chapter One: The Early Years

4. Quoted in Robert Jobson, *Harry's War*. London, UK: John Blake, 2008, p. 23.

5. Quoted in Jobson, *Harry's War*, p. 26.

6. Quoted in Mark Saunders, *Prince Harry: The Biography*. London, UK: John Blake, 2002, p. 18.

7. Quoted in Christopher Andersen, *Diana's Boys*. New York, NY: William Morrow, 2001, p. 63.

8. Quoted in Jobson, *Harry's War*, p. 23.

9. *Harry: The Mysterious Prince*. DVD. Directed by Alan Scales. London, UK: BBC. Worldwide/Infinity, 2005.

10. Quoted in Jobson, *Harry's War*, p. 41.

11. Quoted in Saunders, *Prince Harry*, p. 44.

12. *Harry: The Mysterious Prince*. DVD.

13. *Harry: The Mysterious Prince*. DVD.

14. Quoted in Jobson, *Harry's War*, p. 35.

15. Quoted in Ingrid Seward, *William and Harry*. New York, NY: Arcade, 2003, p. 92.

16. Quoted in Saunders, *Prince Harry*, p. 83.

17. Quoted in Jobson, *Harry's War*, p. 53.

Chapter Two: Growing Up Fast

18. Quoted in Andersen, *Diana's Boys*, p. 122.

19. Quoted in Saunders, *Prince Harry*, p. 58.

20. Quoted in Andersen, *Diana's Boys*, p. 117.

21. Quoted in Andersen, *Diana's Boys*, p. 113.

22. Quoted in Saunders, *Prince Harry*, p. 98.

23. Quoted in Andersen, *Diana's Boys*, p. 22.

24. Quoted in Andersen, *Diana's Boys*, p. 31.

25. Quoted in Christopher Andersen, *After Diana*. New York, NY: Hyperion, 2007, p. 21.

26. Quoted in Saunders, *Prince Harry*, p. 133.

27. Quoted in Matt Lauer, "In Honor of Diana," MSNBC.com, June 27, 2007. www.msnbc.msn.com/id/19190534.

28. *Harry: The Mysterious Prince*. DVD.

29. Quoted in Simon Jeffery, "Prince Harry Urged to Visit Auschwitz," *Guardian*, January 13, 2005. www.guardian.co.uk/uk/2005/jan/13/monarchy.simonjeffery.

30. Quoted in Jobson, *Harry's War*, p. 109.

31. *Harry: The Mysterious Prince*. DVD.

32. Quoted in Andersen, *After Diana*, p. 209.

33. Quoted in Penny Junor, *The Firm*. New York, NY: Thomas Dunne, 2005, p. 414.

Chapter Three: Ten Years in the Military

34. Quoted in "Harry Begins Sandhurst Training," BBC, May 8, 2005. news.bbc.co.uk/2/hi/uk_news/4526077.stm.

35. Quoted in Jobson, *Harry's War*, p. 122.

36. Quoted in "I Was Treated like Dirt at Sandhurst. It Did Me Good," *Telegraph*, September 15, 2005. www.telegraph.co.uk/news/uknews/1498418/I-was-treated-like-dirt-at-Sandhurst.-It-did-me-good.html.

37. Quoted in "I Was Treated like Dirt at Sandhurst. It Did Me Good," *Telegraph*.

38. Quoted in Jobson, *Harry's War*, p. 121.

39. Quoted in Jobson, *Harry's War*, p. 139.

40. "Prince Harry on Afghan Front Line," BBC, February 28, 2008. news.bbc.co.uk/2/hi/7269743.stm.

41. Quoted in Matthew Moore, "Prince Harry Will Not Be Deployed to Iraq," *Telegraph*, May 16, 2007. www.telegraph.co.uk/news/uknews/1551688/Prince-Harry-will-not-be-deployed-to-Iraq.html.

42. Quoted in Jobson, *Harry's War*, p. 148.

43. Quoted in Thomas Harding and Caroline Davies, "Iraq Is Too Dangerous for Harry, Says Army," *Telegraph*, May 17, 2007. www.telegraph.co.uk/news/uknews/1551796/Iraq-is-too-dangerous-for-Harry-says-Army.html.

44. Quoted in "Prince Harry in Afghanistan: The Battlefield Air Controller," *Telegraph*, February 28, 2008. www.telegraph.co.uk/news/uknews/prince-harry/8579275/Prince-Harry-in-Afghanistan-the-Battlefield-Air-Controller.html.

45. Quoted in "Prince Harry in Afghanistan," *Telegraph*.

46. Quoted in Jobson, *Harry's War*, p. xviii.

47. Quoted in Jobson, *Harry's War*, p. xix.

48. Quoted in "Prince Harry in Afghanistan," *Telegraph*.

49. Quoted in "Prince Harry Rejects 'Hero' Label," BBC, March 2, 2008. news.bbc.co.uk/2/hi/uk_news/7273129.stm.

50. Quoted in Rebecca English, "Air Corps Blimey! Chelsy Davy Looks Simply Stunning in Cream Babydoll Dress as Prince Harry Gets His Helicopter Wings," *Daily Mail*, May 7, 2010. www.dailymail.co.uk/tvshowbiz/article-1274439/Prince-Harry-train-Apache-attack-helicopter-pilot.html#ixzz1oRqmPM1q.

Chapter Four: Humanitarian Harry

51. Quoted in Gordon Rayner, "Prince Harry: I Think of My Mother in Everything I Do," *Telegraph*, December, 17, 2010. www.telegraph.co.uk/news/uknews/theroyalfamily/8209168/Prince-Harry-I-think-of-my-mother-in-everything-I-do.html.

52. Quoted in ITN (Independent Television News), *The Forgotten Kingdom: Prince Harry in Lesotho.*

53. Quoted in Sentebale, "About Us: Patrons—The Duke of Sussex," June 3, 2015. sentebale.org/who-we-are/.

54. Quoted in Sentebale, "About Us: Patrons—The Duke of Sussex."

55. Quoted in Prince of Wales, "The Foundation of Prince William and Prince Harry," October 2, 2011. www.princeofwales. gov.uk/newsandgallery/focus/the_foundation_of_prince_ william_ad_prince_harry_570302665.html.

56. Quoted in "Prince Harry: I Sought Counselling After 20 Years of Not Thinking About the Death of My Mother, Diana, and Two Years of Total Chaos in My Life," *Telegraph,* April 19, 2017. www.telegraph.co.uk/news/2017/04/16/ prince-harry-sought-counselling-death-mother-led-two- years-total/?WT.mc_id=tmg_share_tw.

57. Jamie Lowther-Pinkerton, "A Statement by Jamie Lowther-Pinkerton on Prince Harry's Overseas Tour to the Bahamas, Jamaica, Belize and Brazil," Prince of Wales, February 1, 2012. www.princeofwales.gov.uk/ newsandgallery/focus/a_statement_by_jamie_lowther_ pinkerton_on_prince_harry_s_ove_846689140.html.

Chapter Five: Harry Today

58. Quoted in Lauer, "In Honor of Diana."

59. Quoted in Andersen, *After Diana*, p. 210.

60. Quoted in Andersen, *After Diana*, p. 250.

61. Quoted in "Chelsy Is Very Special to Me—She's Amazing," *Telegraph,* September 15, 2005. www.telegraph.co.uk/ news/uknews/1498419/Chelsy-is-very-special-to-me-shes- amazing.html.

62. Quoted in Katie Nicholl, "There's No Pippa Fling, Says '100 Per Cent Single' Prince Harry," *Daily Mail,* June 26, 2011. www.dailymail.co.uk/femail/article-2008197/Theres-Pippa- Middleton-fling-says-100-cent-single-Prince-Harry-Royal- family.html#ixzz1oMH3oGIA.

63. Quoted in Andersen, *After Diana*, p. 227.

64. Quoted in "Royal Wedding: Prince Harry Hails 'Sister' Kate," BBC, December 17, 2010. www.bbc.co.uk/news/uk-12022014.

65. Quoted in Lauer, "In Honor of Diana."

66. Quoted in Sally Pook, "I Don't Want to Change. I Am Who I Am," *Telegraph*, September 15, 2005. www.telegraph.co.uk/news/uknews/1498417/I-dont-want-to-change.-I-am-who-I-am.html.

67. Quoted in Jobson, *Harry's War*, p. 5.

68. Quoted in Lauer, "In Honor of Diana."

69. Quoted in Lauer, "In Honor of Diana."

70. *Harry: The Mysterious Prince*. DVD.

71. Quoted in Angela Levin, "Exclusive: Prince Harry on Chaos After Diana's Death and Why the World Needs 'the Magic' of the Royal Family," *Newsweek*, June 21, 2017. www.newsweek.com/2017/06/30/prince-harry-depression-diana-death-why-world-needs-magic-627833.html.

72. Quoted in Levin, "Exclusive: Prince Harry on Chaos After Diana's Death and Why the World Needs 'the Magic' of the Royal Family."

73. Quoted in Andersen, *After Diana*, pp. 245–246.

Prince Harry Year by Year

1981

Harry's parents, Prince Charles and Lady Diana Spencer, marry at St. Paul's Cathedral in London, in a ceremony that is televised to 750 million people worldwide.

1982

Harry's older brother, Prince William Arthur Philip Louis, is born in London.

1984

Prince Henry Charles Albert David is born on September 15 in the Lindo Wing of St. Mary's Hospital in London; the three-month-old prince is christened by the Archbishop of Canterbury in St. George's Chapel in Windsor Castle.

1989

Prince Harry joins Prince William at Wetherby School, a pre-preparatory school.

1992

Prince Harry joins Prince William at Ludgrove School, Charles and Diana officially separate, and Diana drives to Ludgrove to tell Harry and William the news.

1996

Charles and Diana's divorce is finalized.

1997

Diana is killed in a car crash in Paris; Harry visits South Africa with his father.

1998

Prince Harry joins Prince William at Eton College.

2003

Prince Harry graduates from Eton College; he begins his gap year and visits Australia, where he works as a jackeroo in the outback, and Lesotho, where he works with orphans and is so moved by them that he later produces a documentary about their plight, *The Forgotten Kingdom: Prince Harry in Lesotho.*

2004

Harry is photographed taking a swing at a photographer outside a London nightclub; visits Argentina, where he spends several weeks working on a polo ranch; and begins an on-and-off relationship with Chelsy Davy.

2005

Harry is publicly condemned for wearing a Nazi uniform to a costume party at the home of a friend; serves as a witness, along with Prince William, during his father's wedding to Camilla Parker Bowles; and enters the Royal Military Academy Sandhurst for 44 weeks of training.

2006

Prince Harry completes training at Sandhurst and is commissioned as a second lieutenant in the Blues and Royals of the Household Cavalry Regiment; joins with Prince Seeiso of Lesotho to found the charity Sentebale to help vulnerable children in Lesotho.

2007

The UK Ministry of Defense announces that Harry will accompany his regiment to Iraq, but the army later announces that Harry's deployment has been canceled out of concern for his safety and that of his men; Harry helps plan and host a memorial concert and service to honor Diana's 46th birthday and the 10-year anniversary of her death; and late in the year, he is deployed under a media blackout to Helmand province in southern Afghanistan for military duty.

2008

Prince Harry serves in Afghanistan for 10 weeks before his cover is blown by the media and he is forced to return home; he is promoted to lieutenant and awarded an Operational Service Medal for his service in Afghanistan.

2009

Prince Harry begins training to become an Army Air Corps helicopter pilot; spends eighteen months learning to fly the Apache attack helicopter; and along with William, launches the Foundation of Prince William and Prince Harry.

2011

Prince Harry is promoted to captain; takes part in Walking with the Wounded fundraising expedition to the North Pole; serves as best man at the wedding of William and Kate Middleton; and spends time in the United States for further helicopter training.

2012

Prince Harry completes his Apache helicopter training; makes his first official royal visit on behalf of the queen, visiting Belize, the Bahamas, and Jamaica; and is deployed to Helmand province in Afghanistan as an Apache pilot.

2013

Prince Harry returns from his deployment to Afghanistan.

2014

Prince Harry begins working for HQ London District as a staff officer and creates the Invictus Games.

2016

Prince Harry returns to Lesotho, cofounds the Heads Together campaign with the Duke and Duchess of Cambridge, and begins dating Meghan Markle.

2017

Clarence House announces Prince Harry's engagement to Meghan Markle.

2018

Prince Harry and Meghan Markle are married, making them the Duke and Duchess of Sussex; Kensington Palace announces the Duchess of Sussex is pregnant with her first child.

For More Information

Books

Carroll, Leslie. *American Princess: The Love Story of Meghan Markle and Prince Harry*. New York, NY: Harper Collins, 2018.
This book explores Meghan Markle's life and her relationship with Prince Harry. It includes exclusive information about the royal family.

Life editorial staff. *Diana at 50*. New York, NY: Life, 2011.
This book chronicles the life and death of Diana Spencer. It includes information about and numerous photos of her two children, William and Harry.

Marr, Andrew. *The Real Elizabeth: An Intimate Portrait of Queen Elizabeth II*. New York, NY: Holt, 2012.
This book takes an in-depth look at the life and royal duties of Harry's grandmother, Queen Elizabeth II.

Price, Joann F. *Prince William: A Biography*. Santa Barbara, CA: Greenwood, 2011.
This thorough biography of Prince William also includes in-depth information on Prince Harry and the rest of the royal family.

Websites

Official Website of the British Monarchy
(www.royal.gov.uk)
This website contains extensive information on the entire royal family, including biographies, photos, links, and news stories.

Prince Harry
(topics.nytimes.com/topics/reference/timestopics/people/h/ prince_harry/index.html)
This page on the *New York Times* website provides links to a collection of noteworthy news articles about Prince Harry, as well as outside links.

Prince Harry: People.com
(www.people.com/people/prince_harry/biography)
This site, hosted by *People* magazine, contains a wealth of information on Harry, including a biography and numerous links to news stories about the young prince.

Prince of Wales
(www.princeofwales.gov.uk)
This is the official website for Prince Charles. It contains a section on the Foundation of Prince William and Prince Harry, as well as a section on Harry, with a biography, news, photos, and several links.

Sentebale
(www.sentebale.org)
This is the official website of the charity cofounded by Prince Harry and Prince Seeiso of Lesotho. It contains news stories, information on events, videos, newsletters, and much more. It also contains the documentary *The Forgotten Kingdom*, produced by Harry.

Index

Picture Credits

About the Author

Elizabeth Krajnik is an author and editor residing in Buffalo, New York. She received a bachelor of arts in English from St. Norbert College in De Pere, Wisconsin, and a master of letters in publishing studies from the University of Stirling in Stirling, Scotland. While studying in Scotland, Krajnik interned in the rights department at Canongate Books, publisher of the Booker Prize winner *Life of Pi*. She is the author of *Meghan Markle: American Royal* (Enslow Publishing, 2018) and enjoys learning about the intricacies of British royal life. Other areas of interest include cooking, playing with her dog, and bingeing shows on Netflix.